# Manhood
# GPS

Finding and Following God's Guidance
for Your Adventurous Spirit

PJ McClure

**Manhood GPS: Finding and Following God's Guidance for Your Adventurous Spirit**
ISBN 978-0-9829833-4-8

Editor: Linda A. Schantz

Cover Design: Peppermedia, LLC

Printed in the United States of America

# Dedication

To my brothers in Royal Rangers
for reviving the spirit of adventure
that had long laid dormant in me


To Neil Kennedy
for giving expression
to the five passions of manhood
that I had always known about,
but never could explain

# Table of Contents

★ ★ ★ ★ ★

# Foreword

## BY NEIL KENNEDY

Have you ever watched the television show, *The Amazing Race?*

The globetrotting couples are put in difficult situations and face incredible roadblocks as they make their way around the world. They're given obscure riddles with which they must navigate to unfamiliar destinations. Invariably the adrenaline rush of the race overtakes the common sense of one or more of the couples and they fail to carefully read the clues. They race off without clear directional intent, costing them valuable time and effort.

I've met a lot of men who make the same mistake in life. With an adrenaline rush and an overpowering drive to succeed, they rush through life without getting the directional intent God has for them. When men lean upon their own understanding, they take random paths and roads, usually to discover they've gone far but are completely lost.

**Random isn't direction.**

One of the great attributes about our Father, the God of Abraham, Isaac, and Jacob, is the fact that He doesn't do random. His character is unchanging. He isn't fickle in His approach toward us. He is completely reliable.

Even when Man failed, God was not surprised; He was already prepared for the inevitability that Man would become "lost." On that day in the Garden, rather than having his daily commute with God, the morning ritual that they'd become accustomed to enjoying, Man was withdrawn and shamefully hiding.

Even after Man went off the map, so to speak, God has shown incredible mercy toward us. Again, Man's failure disappointed God but it didn't surprise Him. The Book of Revelation gives us insight that God had prepared the sacrificial Lamb before the foundation of the Earth (Revelation 13:8). This is representative of God's great foresight. He always begins with the end in mind.

This determined end is God's GPS system at work on our behalf.

As Solomon said, *"You can make many plans, but the Lord's purpose will prevail"* (Proverbs 19:21 NLT). Paul also explains this by saying, *"In Him we were also chosen, having been predestined according to the plan of Him who works out everything in conformity with the purpose of His will"* (Ephesians 1:11 NIV).

The fact that God has the foreknowledge of destination doesn't relinquish our responsibilities to navigate faithfully in our commute with Him. We must adhere to the directional commands of the Spirit for our steps to be ordered. You can't decide what you want, make your own plans and then expect God's purpose to prevail in your life.

Your decisions must align with His direction.

In **Manhood GPS,** PJ McClure will help you understand and gain a proficiency in navigating the steps God has ordered for you. This book will be a great help in your daily commute with Him. The accompanying Field Guide will reinforce the lessons learned in this book.

Three men are credited for inventing the modern GPS navigational system: Bradford Parkinson, Roger Easton, and Ivan Getting. *(I mistakenly assumed it was a woman who got tired of driving in circles with the stubborn man who wouldn't pull over for directions.)*

The fact that you're reading this book shows you are wise enough to simply pull over, pause, and ask for guidance. Now, read, listen and get a glimpse of where you're going. The destination is well worth the trip.

*— Neil Kennedy*

# Introduction

## LOST

There is a DNA-level connection between a man and his knowing where to go. In man's earliest days there was no such thing as being lost. Formed from the dirt, wherever the foot of Adam treaded, he was home. Earth was his given domain. All of it!

*...Fill the earth and subdue it.*

*Genesis 1:28 NIV*

So long as he followed the design of his heart, Adam would always be exactly where he was supposed to be. Stop and ask for directions? What for? He walked with the Lord in the cool of the evening and lived under the sound of His voice and guidance (Genesis 3:8).

This communion is God's design: Man taking care of his daily business with his heart turned fully toward God.

It was only after Adam turned his heart toward "being like God" and away from God as his Source that the concept of 'lost' entered the Earth (Genesis 3:5).

It's interesting that Adam was not the one calling out, "Help me! I'm lost! Where am I?" Adam didn't even realize he was lost after the fall. God had to tell him.

*But the Lord God called to the man, "Where are you?"*

*Genesis 3:9 NIV*

God didn't ask the question because He was unsure of Adam's location. He was inviting Adam to realize that his surroundings had changed. In the next moment Adam's entire world shifted and nothing was familiar any more.

**For the first time, man was lost.**

Since Adam, every generation of men has strayed from God's path, entering into the world lost, in desperate need to be found. No matter how hard we try, in our fallen state, we can never find our way through the twists and turns of life.

From the beginning, God never designed that man should be lost. To see the apex of His creation stumbling around directionless, was never God's intent. His plan for us was a surefooted relationship between Creator and His creation. Always on task and enjoying each step. Never drifting or frustrated.

As you read this book, I want you to know that God's original design is still there within you and available for activation. My hope is that you will rediscover His plan for your life in the promises that are revealed in the Bible and explained in these pages. Throughout the years, my personal friends and clients who have received these revelations have discovered that **lost is an option — not a requirement.**

After much prayer, I believe the time has come to put what I've received and tested into writing and ask God to bless every man who reads it. When the men of this generation are back on track, a wave of blessing for the rest of the world will follow.

If men will not admit to their lost state and seek God as their Source and means of direction, the generations to follow will only walk farther away and deeper into darkness. It's up to us to show them how to find their path. To do this, we must learn how to navigate ourselves.

In order to negotiate this life, we need firsthand knowledge of what is going on. The world would have us believe their maps and buy in to their destinations, but God has something different in mind. He wants us to navigate truth and make our decisions as men with His wisdom, not with the arrogance of this age. To do this, we must develop our own *Manhood GPS*.

Building your own GPS to navigate Earth is daunting. You probably don't have access to satellites and global mapping. The resources for such a project are probably out of your reach.

Building your own *Manhood GPS* is a different proposal. Once you become a follower of Jesus, you gain access to everything you need.

For the remainder of this book we will go through turn-by-turn directions to help you understand how to find your way in the world and how to develop your navigational skills to become the authentic man God intended. You will know God better, discern His will more easily and make decisions with a confidence that only comes from the throne room of Heaven.

Think of it... ready access to God's guidance... the Creator of the universe ordering your steps, correcting and reassuring you of the right path. You can navigate the most difficult terrain and make course corrections without everything in life derailing. You can be surefooted and firmly established in His will. Not only is His guidance available to you, it's God's deep desire for you to have it.

> *I will instruct you and teach you in the way you should go; I will counsel you with my loving eye on you. Do not be like the horse or the mule, which have no understanding but must be controlled by bit and bridle or they will not come to you.*
>
> *Psalm 32:8, 9 NIV*

The word picture is plain. We aren't to stand still in stubbornness until we are dragged to where we need to go. We must start our journeys by laying down our selfish agendas and plans in order to open ourselves to what God has for us. Then our love for Him can develop from basic physical obedience into a maturity that allows us to love Him with our minds as well as our hearts (Matthew 22:37).

As we enter this adventure together, please do not check your faculties at the door. Your heart and mind were fashioned and fixed within you by the only One who really knows how to use them. Every page in this book is designed to bring you closer to the Father and into partnership with Holy Spirit, whose chief desire is to make you more like Jesus — to make you an authentic man.

If you are ready to make that move, let's start gathering the pieces you will need to build your *Manhood GPS*.

Your fellow traveler,

— *PJ McClure*

# CHAPTER 1

# On the Road with Grandpa

★ ★ ★ ★ ★

When I was a child, I used to drive around with my
Grandpa Howard. His car was packed with maps and atlases.
They were marked with his previous trips and refolded
meticulously, which is a trick I never learned. He had a
compass suction-cup mounted on the dash and there was
seemingly no place he couldn't find.

As an insurance agent, he would drive all over the
countryside to inspect damage for claims and take pictures of
houses for new accounts. Before leaving for a visit, he would
always open the maps and plan his route. Sometimes though,
the simplest route became more challenging when he had to
translate the maps into our southern-Missouri landscape.

Our neck of the woods was fairly diverse. Especially
when you ventured off of the state highways. County roads
turned into gravel, which in turn might end at an old
logging road or cross a river... without a bridge. Seriously!
Around where I grew up there were, and still are, areas that

show a road traversing a river or a creek that may or may not have a bridge to aid in that crossing.

It was also not uncommon for my grandfather to head toward a client's house to inspect storm damage only to discover the bridge or low-water crossing, which was normally in place, had floated off somewhere downstream. In those moments Grandpa Howard would mutter something like, "It sure would have been nice to know that ahead of time," followed by, "I wonder how on earth I'm going to get there now." Then he'd open up a map and start trying to pull an alternate route together. Within a few minutes, using the same basic steps as always, he had a new course planned and away we went. It might take a lot longer than originally anticipated and sometimes the alternate route was a bust, but he usually found a way to get where he needed to go.

For me, as long as Grandpa was in charge, it felt like an adventure. However, as I got older and found myself in those same kinds of situations, the emotion was considerably different. It's that kind of experience I am focusing on in this book. You know the feeling... **LOST**.

Heading out to a destination that might not be clear and finding yourself at an impasse. Striking out in a direction to go somewhere, and somehow, either because of unfamiliar territory or circumstances out of your control, your best plans are now useless. You find yourself looking around in every direction, *"What do I do now?"*

Today, finding our way around has a different feel than what I learned from Grandpa Howard. His method of maps, notes and compasses feels ancient compared with everyone having mobile GPS in their pockets.

Instead of carefully studying the lay of the land, possible obstacles and landmarks to plan our paths, with the navigational systems we have in our cars and on our phones, we plug in our desired destinations, hit 'Go' and trust the turn-by-turn lady in our devices to guide us safely through.

GPS is not foolproof, but it's an amazing alternative to trying to read a map while driving down the highway.

# THE GIVE AND TAKE

With any technological advance, there is a downside to its use. It may not seem like much of a trade off, but with every move toward reliance on technology comes a move away from the skills and knowledge once required to accomplish the same result.

Years ago when I worked in sales for a radiology company, I traveled all over the country to trade shows, displaying our product line. The company was small and the budget dictated that I drive the equipment to and from the shows myself. I saw parts of the country from the driver's seat of that cargo van that I would have never seen otherwise.

At the time, GPS was still limited to bulky, dashboard units and priced so high that I couldn't afford one. As cool as I thought they were, I still enjoyed planning out my trips with a map. There was something fun about tracing the lines of the roads with my finger predicting what paths would produce the best course on my multi-state routes.

The disadvantage to my method was that a map printed five years earlier would not be able to tell me that I-40 was shut down for six miles west of Nashville. The map also couldn't light up with my exact location and highlight detours to my destination when I unfolded its panels.

The advantages of developing my physical navigating skills showed up in the moments where I could successfully reroute because of familiarity with the area — not because I had traveled it frequently, but because I had studied the map, could discern my location from landmarks, knew my destination, and recognized what direction I needed to go to get there.

With those four tools (map, location, destination and direction) I could find my way through anything. Those were the same four tools Grandpa Howard skillfully used to find his way around.

Even though our aptitude to use these tools has diminished, they're the foundation of the technology we enjoy in our GPS units today. From the comfort of our motorized transportation we speak our desire. The voice-recognition system captures the information, translates it into possible matches, shows us options and prepares to navigate. We then choose our route based on our mood or timeframe, and away we go.

It isn't uncommon for us to travel 300 to 500 miles in a day with no more skill or knowledge than what it takes to speak the name of a destination and obey instructions given to us by a disembodied voice. We travel throughout the world, much of it unknown to us personally, and think nothing of it.

The concept really is amazing to think about. Voyagers throughout the centuries risked their lives and set out on expeditions of only a few hundred miles with no maps or with only crude drawings of their surroundings. They had to rely on their connection to the terrain to keep their bearings. Only the most skillful had success. Those who returned alive gained an intimate knowledge of the explored land. That knowledge became a part of their life, their story.

## LOSING TOUCH

In recent years I've taken GPS-guided trips where I couldn't tell you anything about the ground I covered. When all I had to do was listen to instructions, I lost my knowledge and appreciation for the terrain. The road became a means to an end instead of the very thing on which I lived.

Modern Christianity is experiencing something very similar. We have loads of pioneers who had serious work to do as they discovered who God was and what He was like. If we only look at those listed in the "Hall of Faith" from Hebrews 11, the miles of spiritual ground they covered is staggering. Think of Abraham and all the new ground he covered as God revealed Himself. Abraham was moved to the point of being willing to sacrifice his own son because he firmly believed God would raise him from the dead. **Now, that was new territory!**

Every hero of the faith faced some new or deepened revelation of God, and we have a written record of their experiences to chart our own journeys. And some of the greatest minds in Judeo-Christian thought have studied those experiences and helped us understand God better through the benefit of their own revelations.

Today we have more available information about the things of God than we could ever consume. Instead of pouring through scripture and immersing ourselves in prayer; however, we often see what others think and plot our course with their recommended routes. Sermons, podcasts, books, commentaries... We enjoy the benefit of the advanced thought of others. Yet our own level of personal intimacy, knowledge and skill regarding God and His kingdom is diminished.

Don't get me wrong. God wants us to enjoy the great advancements that have come about since the days scripture was recorded, but He doesn't want the efforts of the men before us to replace the work we must put in for ourselves. He's not opposed to our use of a *Manhood GPS*; He just wants us to build our own.

This trend of knowing God through the experiences of others is at the heart of the crisis affecting manhood today. Authentic manhood is lost because generations of men have given over their personal relationships with Almighty God and exploration of His kingdom in exchange for hearing an occasional story told by someone who is actually living the journey.

We're so enamored with modern conveniences that we've allowed a godless society to reduce the Creator of the *universe to theme-park status. "Feel free to roam and explore! Enjoy the rides. Just don't go beyond the fence. Leave it all behind when you travel into the rest of your life. This stuff doesn't belong out there!"*

The truths and laws of God, which govern a righteous life, are not convenient for a society bent on redefining morals to what feels good. God's design of authentic manhood is even less convenient in a culture that values turning your head and tolerance more than standing up for what is right.

Inconvenient or not, it is time for us to get started.

# CHAPTER 2

# The Right Map

★ ★ ★ ★ ★

In 2008, my wife and I planned a trip to Florida with four friends. We decided to take two cars. Most of the luggage went with us, and our four friends piled into the other car.

Preparing for the twelve-hour drive from southern Missouri to Panama City Beach, I studied the maps. I had driven most of the route multiple times, but there was a stretch of road that had recently been turned into a new section of interstate highway. Since a big chunk of the trip would be during the night, I thought it wise to know as much of the route ahead of time.

When we met up on the day of the trip, Denise, one of my wife's friends, told us she had a GPS unit installed in her car for work travel. "Navi," as she called it, was a unit that required updates via CDs mailed to the user from the manufacturer. Assured that the updates were current, I let them lead.

A few hours into the trip we approached Memphis. Having driven this section a dozen or more times, I got a strange feeling about our travel lane a mile out. "We aren't in the correct lane," I told my wife. "We should be in the far right lane to get where we need to go."

But instead of calling and trying to have a discussion on the phone, we trusted Navi and followed. Twenty minutes later we found ourselves surrounded by houses and street signs. We finally saw a gas station and stopped. As it turned out, Navi had plotted our course through a couple of residential neighborhoods instead of on the major highways. I asked the gas station attendant how to get back to the road we should have been on and then led the way out of town.

The new stretch of interstate was easy enough to find and it seemed as if the rough patch was behind us. We would stick to this road for almost 200 miles before our next turn, so it didn't bother me when our friends decided to pass and take the lead again.

With more than a hundred miles to go before our next turn, our lead vehicle exited off the highway. "Maybe they need a bathroom break," my wife commented. But they drove right past the gas station and on to a poorly marked county road.

"Are you kidding?!" was my immediate reaction.

Giving them very little leash this time, I asked my wife to call and tell them to pull over at the next opportunity. And there, outside Captain's Catfish House somewhere in northern Mississippi, I officially revoked Navi's navigational privileges!

The GPS had no trouble pinpointing our location or trying to steer us toward our destination. The problem was that it didn't have a map for the path we were traveling! Since turning onto the new highway, the *"You Are Here"* dot had been floating in gray space. *"No Road"* was the constant message and Navi kept telling our friends to turn at every exit.

Fortunately because I had studied the maps, I knew where we were headed and had confidence in our direction.

## TRAVELING BLIND

*If people can't see what God is doing, they stumble all over themselves; but when they attend to what He reveals, they are most blessed.*

*Proverbs 29:18 MSG*

Navigation in our natural world has four major components, which when combined, give it the accuracy and usefulness we need — **a map, knowledge of our current location, a clear destination, and a means of direction.** These four things are necessary for GPS technology to work as it was designed. Our trip to Florida made the importance of all four pieces obvious to me. Navi had three of the four components, but the lack of an updated map could have thrown the entire journey into a tailspin. With all its satellite technology and digital magic, without a map, GPS is worthless. Everything it does depends upon the map.

## A WORD ABOUT MAPS

A map is a two-dimensional representation of our three-dimensional world. A map of the Appalachian Mountains is **not** the Appalachian Mountains. It simply represents the mountains in a way that we can see an overview of the characteristics and the lay of the land.

A map is initially based on someone else's collected experience. Nothing can be mapped until someone gets in the middle of it and records their experiences, complete with mistakes, discoveries, successful paths and places to avoid. The more experiences collected the better.

Journeys are all about gaining our own experiences with the help of the maps provided by others. The better we become at studying and interpreting maps, the more successful our own journeys will be.

I have heard the Bible called many things in Christian circles, but my favorite, and I think the most accurate description is to call it a map.

*The* Map.

"A map of what?" is the most frequent question I hear after making that statement.

To answer that I have to say that I don't think it's just a map for our lives or simply an instruction manual for how we should live. Yes, I believe the Bible is our authoritative rule of faith and conduct, but I further believe its primary purpose is much deeper than that. In fact, **I would suggest that the Holy Bible, which we base our faith and lives upon, is a map of God Himself.** I could also say it is a map of the kingdom of Heaven.

> *For in Him we live and move and have our being.*
>
> *Acts 17:28 NIV*

The entirety of our existence is based on our relationship with God and in deepening that relationship by seeking His revelation. In the last book of the Bible, we see a picture that captures this notion for me.

> *Also in front of the throne there was what looked like a sea of glass, clear as crystal. In the center, around the throne, were four living creatures, and **they were covered with eyes, in front and in back**... Each of the four living creatures had six wings and was covered with eyes all around... Day and night they never stop saying: "Holy, holy, holy is the Lord God Almighty, who was, and is, and is to come."*
>
> *Revelation 4:6, 8 NIV (Author's emphasis)*

Think about that for a moment. These four creatures were covered with eyes, in front and in back. Why? All they do for eternity is gaze upon God. They are covered with eyes so they don't miss anything about Him, and their response is to never stop saying, *"Holy, holy, holy is the Lord God Almighty."*

**For all eternity God will continue to reveal more about Himself and we will be in continuous and unceasing awe.**

There are even things of God that cannot be revealed to us in this life because they won't have application until we are fully in eternity with Him!

That said, God wants us to know all we can about Him now.

> *It is the glory of God to conceal a matter; to search out a matter is the glory of kings.*
>
> *Proverbs 25:2 NIV*

As we dive into this concept of *Manhood GPS,* understanding the ground we traverse and the importance of our map is our top priority. We must become experts at navigating the kingdom — experts in knowing God.

## READING THE MAP

I have spoken with countless people who don't understand the Bible or its role in our lives today.

"It's hard to read."

"How can I apply what God did thousands of years ago to what's happening today?"

"I don't see how it is relevant."

There is no doubt that cultural relevance often gets in the way when we attempt to make a direct connection between many of the stories we see in Scripture and our modern walk. The enemy capitalizes on that gap and casts doubt in our minds about the accuracy and application of God's Word. We have to adjust our perspective to understand and receive revelation today.

My friend, and the founder of *FivestarMan,* Neil Kennedy, uses the triad of **precept, principle and practice** in studying and teaching Scripture. You will see this pattern throughout this book and can use it as you study the Bible to understand how God's response to an orphaned, hot-headed, exiled murderer in ancient Egypt (Moses), for example, has specific application to your decisions as a man today.

The triad of revelation works like this:

**Precept** — *A spoken commandment or rule for order; a divine oracle to prescribe wisdom*

Though they are rarely the detailed and specific direction we want, precepts reveal the unchanging attributes of God that help us establish moral character and daily habits.

**Principle** — *The interpretation of the precept; used to understand the results or consequences of following or departing from the precept*

This is where we begin seeking a natural context to apply God's eternal precepts. It's a wonderful thing to experience the moment of clarity where something eternal becomes tangible.

**Practice** — *Applying the principle to a specific moment and situation of your life*

Most people know the principles of physical fitness and basic nutrition, but to actually apply those principles is a different story. Without the practice of the principle, the precept goes ignored.

Now let's go back to the example of Moses to understand how this works.

When the nation of Israel was brought out of 400 years of captivity in Egypt, they had undoubtedly picked up many of the religious and cultural influences from their pagan captures. To give their complete allegiance to God, they had to be fully liberated from Egypt physically, mentally and spiritually.

God began re-establishing His precepts through the various moral and ceremonial laws He handed down through Moses. Some of the laws were communicated in a way that we may not understand culturally, so our job is to find the precept, the principle and the practice.

In his book, **Speaking The Father's Blessing,** Neil Kennedy gives a great example.

> The Bible says, "Do not muzzle an ox while it is treading out the grain" (Deuteronomy 25:4). This is a precept established to govern the conduct of people while an ox is working in the field. Few of us own an ox, though, so on the surface it would seem this precept is not applicable to us. But the principle behind this precept is that a laborer should receive nourishment from his labor. The Apostle Paul used this precept and principle to encourage the Church regarding the financial support he was given from those who were the beneficiaries of his labor (1 Corinthians 9:9). Paul later applied it to ministerial compensation in the Church (1 Timothy 5:18).
>
> The precept is the established authority. The principle behind it is the interpretation of the precept. The practice is the application of the principle into daily life.

With this **precept-principle-practice** framework firmly under our belts, let's begin looking at our map and see what's revealed about God's desire for us to know Him better.

# CHAPTER 3

# Following the Map

★ ★ ★ ★ ★

Analogies are wonderful teaching tools. Through analogy we can take a complex, sometimes-indescribable concept and make sense of it by comparing the unknown to something we know.

In comparing the Bible to a map, and God and the kingdom of Heaven to the land, I hope to bring a little bit of perspective to our interaction with the Divine. Please note, however, that similar to all analogies, even this comparison will eventually breakdown. God is so much greater than the most pristine and beautiful landscape and His kingdom beyond our comprehension that we cannot compare Him accurately to anything because He has no equal.

And yet, He still desires for us to know Him.

There are patterns and references throughout Scripture telling us to know God better. You will see them throughout our journey here and probably recognize even more of them

in your private study from now on. For our purposes in this
book, I want to start with two key passages:

> *I have not stopped giving thanks for you,*
> *remembering you in my prayers. I keep asking*
> *that the God of our Lord Jesus Christ, the*
> *glorious Father, may give you the Spirit of*
> *wisdom and revelation, **so that you may know***
> ***Him better**. I pray that the eyes of your heart*
> *may be enlightened in order that you may*
> *know the hope to which He has called you, the*
> *riches of his glorious inheritance in His holy*
> *people, and His incomparably great power for*
> *us who believe....*
>
> Ephesians 1:16-19 NIV (Author's emphasis)

> *For this reason, since the day we heard about*
> *you, we have not stopped praying for you. We*
> *continually **ask God to fill you with the***
> ***knowledge of His will** through all the wisdom*
> *and understanding that the Spirit gives, so*
> *that you may live a life worthy of the Lord and*
> *please Him in every way: bearing fruit in*
> *every good work, **growing in the knowledge***
> ***of God**, being strengthened with all power*
> *according to his glorious might so that you*
> *may have great endurance and patience.*
>
> Colossians 1:9-11 NIV (Author's emphasis)

In these verses we see consistent themes in the Apostle
Paul's desire for the Early Church — *"know Him better," "the
knowledge of His will," "the knowledge of God."* This is a
big topic in the kingdom! We see God establishing the
importance of this in how He interacted with the early
fathers of the faith. We can go all the way back to the
beginning and see God sharing His attributes and nature
with man — with Adam and Eve all the way through Noah —
but we really get to see His desire to be known and have a
relationship starting with Abraham.

In the life of Abraham, The Lord begins revealing His
heart. He calls Abraham to separate himself and follow His
divine leading (Genesis 12:1-9). God is faithful in all He

promises, even when Abraham's behavior is not the best (Genesis 12:10-18). The God of Heaven and Earth interacts with man on a level where Abraham can ask for mercy upon a corrupted city and God hears his plea (Genesis 18:16-33). Most importantly for our study, God guided and directed Abraham by revelation of His nature.

Through every turn we see that by His mouth or hand, God motivated, corrected and steadied Abraham by revealing Himself and how He felt about Abraham's actions and heart. By knowing more and more of God, Abraham came to a point of confidence and faith that allowed him to offer anything God asked, knowing that God was faithful to keep His promises (Genesis 22:1-19).

By becoming intimately familiar with the nature of God, Abraham was able to believe for a promise that extended beyond his own lifetime and to pass that faith on to his son (Genesis 24:7). Later, we see the Lord continuing this revelation to Isaac.

> *The Lord appeared to Isaac and said, "Do not go down to Egypt; live in the land where I tell you to live. Stay in this land for a while, and I will be with you and will bless you. For to you and your descendants I will give all these lands and will confirm the oath I swore to your father Abraham. I will make your descendants as numerous as the stars in the sky and will give them all these lands, and through your offspring all nations on earth will be blessed, because Abraham obeyed me and did everything I required of him, keeping my commands, my decrees and my instructions."*
>
> *Genesis 26:2-5 NIV*

God invested in Abraham and revealed Himself through His promises and actions. Then God gave a new level of revelation to Isaac for the second generation. In essence the message was, "I'm the same God as I was with your father. He was the first to walk in the way I commanded him; you will be the second. But because of your father's obedience and faith, you will not start at the beginning. I will bless you because of him, so you will see that your life extends beyond you."

This is a new perspective on the land, a new vantage point. Faithful obedience is a generational matter to God. When we're truly pursuing the heart of God and living up to His expectations for us as men, we'll believe and act for a vision beyond our own lives.

Continuing with the legacy, Isaac's son Jacob also began to understand this precept in his first encounter with the living God.

> There above it stood the LORD, and he said: "I am the LORD, the God of your father Abraham and the God of Isaac. I will give you and your descendants the land on which you are lying. Your descendants will be like the dust of the earth, and you will spread out to the west and to the east, to the north and to the south. All peoples on earth will be blessed through you and your offspring. I am with you and will watch over you wherever you go, and I will bring you back to this land. I will not leave you until I have done what I have promised you."
>
> *Genesis 28:13-15 NIV*

Does that sound familiar? It's the same promise God gave Abraham and Isaac. Jacob had inherited the promise of his fathers.

Note Jacob's reaction to all of this:

> When Jacob awoke from his sleep, he thought, "Surely the LORD is in this place, and I was not aware of it." He was afraid and said, "How awesome is this place! This is none other than the house of God; this is the gate of heaven."
>
> *Genesis 28:16, 17 NIV*

Instantly, through the revelation of God about Himself, Jacob knew the lay of the land. He knew exactly where he was and what it meant! This is our model. God reveals Himself to each generation by reminding them who He was to the previous generations. Our revelation builds on their experiences because there's always something new to see and learn about His unchanging nature.

To set up the rest of our journey, let's look at the end of Jacob's life, when his name was changed to Israel and his family was in Egypt enjoying great prosperity because of God's hand on his son Joseph.

> *Then he blessed Joseph and said, "May the God before whom my fathers Abraham and Isaac walked faithfully, the God who has been my shepherd all my life to this day, the Angel who has delivered me from all harm — may He bless these boys. May they be called by my name and the names of my fathers Abraham and Isaac, and may they increase greatly on the earth."*
>
> *Genesis 48:15, 16 NIV*

In the presence of one of his sons and two grandsons, Israel passed on the map. They had undoubtedly heard him tell the generational stories of how God treated their ancestors and his own personal journey. With this blessing, they understood Who would be with them and how they were to travel through life as descendants.

Four hundred years later, that blessing was still carried on, as the nation of Israel *"increased abundantly, multiplied and grew exceedingly mighty"* (Exodus 1:7 NKJV); however, they had been enslaved by the Egyptians and were in need of deliverance.

Yes, they were a multitude, but they were not where they belonged. In many ways, they were lost. It is against this backdrop that we see the greatest scriptural example of the elements which comprise our *Manhood GPS*.

# SUCCESSION

Through miraculous circumstances and against all earthly odds, an Israelite child named Moses was raised in the house of Pharaoh. His own mother nursed and cared for him and was able to pass on to him the knowledge of her God — the God of Abraham, Isaac and Jacob (Exodus 1:15–2:10).

Even though Moses had his mother's map of God, when the time came for him to be called to deliver Israel, God reinforced the lay of the land Moses knew. In front of the burning bush, God made sure He was known.

> *"Do not come any closer," God said. "Take off your sandals, for the place where you are standing is holy ground." Then he said, "I am the God of your father, the God of Abraham, the God of Isaac and the God of Jacob." At this, Moses hid his face, because he was afraid to look at God. The Lord said, "I have indeed seen the misery of my people in Egypt. I have heard them crying out because of their slave drivers, and I am concerned about their suffering. So I have come down to rescue them from the hand of the Egyptians and to bring them up out of that land into a good and spacious land, a land flowing with milk and honey...."*

> *Exodus 3:5-8 NIV*

God was going to do amazing things through Moses. God and Moses would become friends and have an unequaled relationship, and God began it all by giving Moses a map. In essence He said, "I am God: A personal God — the God you already know — the God of Abraham, Isaac and Jacob. I am your God, Moses. I am what you need to be concerned with, not the natural landscape around you. You need to know Me, and the rest will come into alignment."

When Jesus said, *"Seek first His kingdom and His righteousness, and all these things will be given to you as well,"* (Matthew 6:33 NIV) this is what He meant. **Our world**

**is God.** If we know that world intimately and give our full attention there, the things of this lesser world will come, as a result.

On the doorstep of the greatest undertaking in history, God told Moses to know Him. The success of the Exodus, even in light of the nation's disobedience, is due to Moses continually seeking God. Throughout Moses' life, we see revelation after revelation about God.

And when we see the final step toward the possession of the Promised Land after the death of Moses, the legacy of map giving continued.

> *After the death of Moses the servant of the Lord, the Lord said to Joshua son of Nun, Moses' aide: "Moses my servant is dead. Now then, you and all these people, get ready to cross the Jordan River into the land I am about to give to them — to the Israelites. I will give you every place where you set your foot,* **as I promised Moses.** *Your territory will extend from the desert to Lebanon, and from the great river, the Euphrates — all the Hittite country — to the Mediterranean Sea in the west. No one will be able to stand against you all the days of your life.* **As I was with Moses, so I will be with you;** *I will never leave you nor forsake you. Be strong and courageous, because you will lead these people to inherit* **the land I swore to their ancestors to give them.** *Be strong and very courageous. Be careful to* **obey all the law my servant Moses gave you;** *do not turn from it to the right or to the left, that you may be successful wherever you go. Keep this Book of the Law always on your lips; meditate on it day and night, so that you may be careful to do everything written in it. Then you will be prosperous and successful. Have I not commanded you? Be strong and courageous. Do not be afraid; do not be discouraged, for* **the Lord your God will be with you wherever you go."**

> *Joshua 1:1-9 NIV (Author's emphasis)*

This entire opening discourse between God and Joshua is about knowing God. Not only did God reiterate the elements that had been passed down through Moses, but God began Joshua's journey as the leader with new promises.

*"No one will be able to stand against you all the days of your life."*

*"Keep this Book of the Law always on your lips; meditate on it day and night."*

*"Be strong and courageous. Do not be afraid; do not be discouraged."*

Joshua was the protégé of Moses, so he would have been the most familiar with how God interacted with Moses. Joshua knew the promises of obedience and the consequences of disobedience like no one else in all of Israel, and still God reminded him: "As long as you are focused on Me, you have nothing to fear."

In this way, Joshua continued the legacy of God's revelation to us. Building upon each progressive generation, we receive a map of incredible detail. From beginning to end, the Bible shows us the attributes of God, what He expects and how He responds to His creation.

In the pages of His Word, we find that:

- God is a personal spirit
- God is all powerful
- God is ever present
- God knows everything
- God is sovereign
- God is holy
- God is absolute truth
- God is righteous

- God is just

- God is love

- God is merciful

- God is faithful

- God never changes

In the context of what we are discussing, I think that last one in this list is especially important. We read over and over, "I'm the same God. I do not change."

When I know God based on His interactions with others, even if those interactions took place thousands of years ago, I can plan my path accordingly. Their journey was different than mine, but God is the same. In the same way the knowledge of mountains, valleys and rivers based on maps created by others allows me to navigate successfully, the knowledge I receive about God from other sources gives me confidence for my life today.

*(Author's Note: The corresponding Field Guide to this book will walk you through a study of all of the attributes in our list and the places they're found in Scripture.)*

Through the example of His life and in His teachings, Jesus gave us more detailed maps. Many parables start with a variation of, *"The kingdom of Heaven is like..."* or *"The Father is like...".*

Everything Jesus did pointed back to the Father. Now, through personal revelation, the Holy Spirit points back to Jesus. In our study and meditation of Scripture we receive more details for our own journeys. We need only ask the Holy Spirit, "How does this apply to me in my situation?" and listen for the reply.

All these things point back to our keynote scriptures.

> *...That the God of our Lord Jesus Christ, the glorious Father, may give you the Spirit of*

*wisdom and revelation, **so that you may know
him better.** I pray that the eyes of your heart
may be enlightened in order that you may
know the hope to which he has called you, the
riches of his glorious inheritance in his holy
people, and his incomparably great power for
us who believe....*

*Ephesians 1:16-19 NIV (Author's emphasis)*

*...We continually **ask God to fill you with the
knowledge of his will** through all the wisdom
and understanding that the Spirit gives, so
that you may live a life worthy of the Lord and
please him in every way: bearing fruit in
every good work, **growing in the knowledge
of God**, being strengthened with all power
according to his glorious might so that you
may have great endurance and patience.*

*Colossians 1:9-11 NIV (Author's emphasis)*

We must know Him better and be filled with the
knowledge of His will so that we can grow in the knowledge
of God. With every step we gain knowledge of Him, and our
ability to navigate this world for His glory increases.

But we still need a few more pieces to really make it
work. Discovering our starting point is next.

# CHAPTER 4

# Location, Location, Location

★ ★ ★ ★ ★

Imagine for a moment that you woke up and have no idea where you are. Perhaps you're in a wilderness with dense vegetation and you can't see more than twenty feet in any direction. By any definition, you could be called "lost."

Imagine then that things really get weird when you hear a Tarzan yell and I come swooping in on a vine and plop down in front of you. With a wink and a nod, I hand you a map of the area and swing off into my wilderness bliss.

Aside from how cool I think it would be to swing through the forest on a vine, what would have been accomplished in this scenario? You were lost and I gave you a map.

*Now what?*

A map by itself is not very useful unless you use it to start a fire. In order to use a map effectively it has to have context. The first thing you need to establish is your current location.

Without knowing where you are, nothing on a map will make sense.

Shortly after turning sixteen, I went on a trip with a few friends to watch a basketball tournament. Thinking our normal route of highways might take too long, I decided to cut cross country on some rather sketchy roads.

When night fell and we still hadn't found the route we intended to come out on, I stopped and pulled out the map. "Here's where we want to be," I pointed out easily, "but how do we get there?"

Even having a general idea of our whereabouts was not very helpful because the direction we needed to travel depended on our actual location. From one place, going north would have gotten us there. From another, our course would have been toward the east.

Fortunately we met someone on the road who knew where we were and they helped us find our spot on the map. With that information, the map came into focus and we knew what was required to get back on track.

## YOUR SPIRITUAL LOCATION

Our physical location is the critical piece in navigation since all of the other pieces get their meaning from it. The path to our destination and the direction of travel are both dependent upon where we start. Taking our spiritual life into consideration, our understanding of our current position is just as important.

After His crucifixion, two of Jesus' disciples were traveling to a village called Emmaus, discussing all that had occurred. These guys were lost. They had studied Scripture under Jesus' guidance and had grown to believe that He was the Messiah (Luke 24:13-21). Familiarity with the map was not their problem.

Jesus appeared to them and, "Beginning with Moses and all the Prophets, He explained to them what was said in all the Scriptures concerning Himself." It was not until then that they were able to see where they were in terms of the overall story (Luke 24:27 NIV). They found their location on the map.

We see it when Philip was called to *"Go south to the road — the desert road — that goes down from Jerusalem to Gaza"* (Acts 8:26 NIV). There he met the Ethiopian eunuch reading Scripture, and asked him the question we are considering right now.

> ... *"Do you understand what you are reading?" Philip asked.*
>
> *"How can I," he said, "unless someone explains it to me?"*
>
> *Acts 8:30-31 NIV*

This man had a map and very much wanted to know how to navigate, but he did not know his starting point. By the grace of God, Philip was able to show him his spiritual position and the eunuch decided to follow Jesus as a result.

But how does this narrative apply to us today?

A few clues in the passage let us know the eunuch's status. He came to Jerusalem to worship, so we know he was Jewish, either converted on his own or born to converted parents. He was an official in a royal court and, therefore, familiar with protocol and privilege. And he was a eunuch, which has as much implication as anything.

Though we do not know the details of how he became a eunuch (most likely meaning he had no testicles), his statement in verse 31 about needing someone to teach him tells us that he was not allowed inside the Temple, according to the ceremonial law in Deuteronomy 23:1. Given the exclusionary attitudes of many of the teachers of the Law in that day, it stands to reason this Ethiopian official was an outcast in a spiritual sense.

Even though his earthly identity was that of an educated, responsible and valued official, his spiritual identity was second-class at best. When Philip revealed the Gospel of Jesus to him in Scripture, this previously excluded, second-class citizen realized he was much more! He had access to the spiritual privilege of the elite.

> ... *"Look, here is water. What can stand in the way of my being baptized?"*
>
> *Acts 8:36 NIV*

My loose paraphrase: "According to the work of Jesus, I am now ceremonially clean and can enter the assembly of the Lord. My identity has changed and now I know what to do next!"

**This is our principle: In the spiritual realm, our location is our identity, and our identity is based on our proximity to God.** The eunuch had resigned himself to a spiritual life of distance, looking in from the outside, but in the good news of Jesus he saw himself in a new way. Instead of feeling as if he were less than a man due to his physical state, he could be baptized into Jesus and have a new closeness with the Father.

# THE POINT OF ATTACK

Your identity is precious. We know how valuable identity is in the natural realm by the constant reminders of how dishonest dirt bags want to steal it. We can also gauge its value in the spiritual realm by how often it's attacked.

From the beginning, satan tried to gain an upper hand by attacking man's identity in the Garden. There was no forceful assault or bribery to get control. He simply, yet cleverly, went after the identity given to Adam and Eve.

"The fully privileged creation of God," could have been the identity our first ancestors walked in. Given full reign and access to all of the goodness of God, they lived in total privilege as children of the Ultimate Ruler. Everything that was His was theirs to enjoy.

But satan came in and attacked the focal point of their identity. *"Did God really say, 'You must not eat from any tree in the garden'?"* (Genesis 3:1) His weapon was doubt and deceit. This father of all lies knew that Adam and Eve were beloved and trusted by God, but the devil wanted them to doubt. At first it seemed that Eve was firm in her identity, but the enemy's lies took a toll.

> *The woman said to the serpent, "We may eat fruit from the trees in the garden, but God did say, 'You must not eat fruit from the tree that is in the middle of the garden, and you must not touch it, or you will die.'"*
>
> *"You will not certainly die," the serpent said to the woman. "For God knows that when you eat from it your eyes will be opened, and you will be like God, knowing good and evil."*
>
> *Genesis 3:2-5 NIV*

"You aren't trusted." "God wants to keep you ignorant." "You don't need Him as your provider." "You can have all the knowledge yourself." The devil did not tell them overt lies. He simply repositioned truthful statements to cause Adam and Eve to doubt their relationship with God. They lost track of who they were and distanced themselves through disobedience.

## LOST AND FOUND

In terms of identity, there aren't many men in Scripture who could have been more confused than Moses. Born a Hebrew slave, adopted into Pharaoh's house, nursed by his birth mother who taught him about God, raised in the privilege of Egyptian royalty among many gods, Moses was inclined to defend his native people who were enslaved by his adoptive people. In so doing, Moses killed an Egyptian and was on the run from everyone.

Surrounded by confusion, Moses may not have had the most solid identity when God issued the call for him to free a nation. Faced with a miraculous burning bush, we see his identity crisis surface.

> *But Moses said to God, "Who am I that I should go to Pharaoh and bring the Israelites out of Egypt?"*
>
> *Exodus 3:11 NIV (Author's emphasis)*

*"Who am I?"* Moses asks. This is not just a question of worth, but also a question of identity. Imagine the thoughts running through his head. "I'm a Hebrew, raised in Pharaoh's house, now rejected and on the run for my life because I'm a murderer. Who am I to go into Egypt and do anything?!"

The part of the story we need to focus on is God's answer.

> *And God said, "**I will be with you.** And this will be the sign to you that it is I who have sent you: When you have brought the people out of Egypt, you will worship God on this mountain."*
>
> *Exodus 3:12 NIV (Author's emphasis)*

Given just a little study, we can come up with a pretty convincing argument as to why Moses was God's chosen man. All of the things that contributed to his identity crises were actually reasons why he was uniquely qualified to be the ambassador and leader.

- Hebrew bloodline

- Egyptian, royal education

- No place left for him in Egypt

Moses was the only person on the planet with his unique skill set and experiences. It really makes perfect sense as to why he would be the one, but that very convincing argument is not what God used to assure him.

**"I will be with you."**

Right away God wants Moses to know the question, *"Who am I?"* is not about what we possess in earthly terms; it's about our proximity to Him.

Let that sink in deeply, because it took a few tries for Moses to get it. I think God wants us to get it, too.

> *Moses said to God, "Suppose I go to the Israelites and say to them, 'The God of your fathers has sent me to you,' and they ask me, 'What is his name?' Then what shall I tell them?"*
>
> *God said to Moses, "I am who I am. This is what you are to say to the Israelites: 'I AM has sent me to you.'"*
>
> *Exodus 3:13-14 NIV*

Moses was asking questions about credibility and identity, and God essentially said, "Your credibility is that you are with Me."

Fortunately for our lesson, Moses still did not understand the power of God's presence. God showed Moses that he could go with what was already in his possession (Exodus 4:1-9). God convinced Moses that His abilities were enough (Exodus 4:10-17) and eventually Moses set out on the journey back to Egypt because he understood that his identity came from being close to God.

# PROXIMITY

David was identified by those around him as the youngest son of Jesse and only worthy to tend the family's sheep. But David found his true identity in the pasture as a lover and worshipper of God.

There was strength in this spiritual identity that caused David to defend everything entrusted to his care. When a lion or bear came to take a sheep, David killed the predators and protected his father's flock.

When Samuel came to anoint one of Jesse's sons as the next king of Israel, David wasn't even invited. Only after God rejected the rest of his brothers was David brought in from the pasture to receive the anointing to rule (1 Samuel 16:9-13).

The most fascinating part about David's sense of identity was what happened after his anointing ceremony. Instead of trying to become king right away or assuming the attitude he was deserving of the position, David went back to tending the sheep. We don't see him again in Scripture until he was called into the service of King Saul (1 Samuel 16:19). With humility and excellence, David maintained his identity and closeness with the Lord by honoring Him in everything.

The victory over Goliath gives an even better account of how David derived his identity from his proximity to God. Everyone in the Israelite camp was terrified of Goliath, but David questioned Goliath's identity.

> *"Who is this uncircumcised Philistine that he should defy the armies of the living God?"*
>
> *1 Samuel 17:26 (Author's emphasis)*

In other words, "This guy isn't close to God! We are!" It's that strength which gave David victory over the giant. By focusing on where he stood in relationship to God, the youngest son of Jesse was firm in his identity.

As king, however, the life of David gives us examples of what can happen when we forget our identities. The most obvious is his sin with Bathsheba.

David had lived most of his life from his identity in God — a lover and worshipper of the Lord, a servant, a warrior and a just king — but then we find a troubling passage.

> *In the spring, at the time when kings go off to war, David sent Joab out with the king's men*

*and the whole Israelite army. They destroyed*
*the Ammonites and besieged Rabbah. But*
*David remained in Jerusalem.*

*2 Samuel 11:1 NIV*

The implications are clear. David was the warrior-king and kings went off to war. David stayed behind and laid aside his identity. Men are designed for purposeful action. Things come undone when we get comfortable and complacent. David fell into boredom, adultery, deception and murder (2 Samuel 11:2-26). This was not who David was in the Lord, but it took a strong rebuke from God to bring him back to his identity (2 Samuel 12:1-30).

David made mistakes but he's remembered as a man after God's own heart (Acts 13:22). You can't be much closer to someone than to be "after his or her heart."

We must remember **where** we are by knowing **who** we are, and who we are is determined by **how close** we are to God. Identity is a matter of proximity.

So let's figure out where you are with God.

# CHAPTER 5

# **Where Are You?**

★ ★ ★ ★ ★

The ultimate example of the power of identity is Jesus. As Immanuel, God with us, He faced the same weaknesses we do, yet He never lost sight of who He was or where He was in God (Hebrews 4:15).

It's conceivable that no one has ever been surer of His identity than Jesus. His mother would have told Him the story of her visitation from the angel, her immaculate conception and the host of peculiar visitors they received. At age twelve, Jesus clearly identified His position in God by stating that He *"had to be in His Father's house"* when His earthly parents found Him in the Temple (Luke 2:49).

If that wasn't clear enough, the Father declared the identity of His Son publicly.

> *As soon as Jesus was baptized, he went up out of the water. At that moment heaven was opened, and he saw the Spirit of God descending like a dove and alighting on him.*

*And a voice from heaven said, "This is My Son,
whom I love; with him I am well pleased."*

*Matthew 3:16,17 NIV*

With this scene as the prelude, Jesus' identity was still
what satan chose to attack. After forty days of fasting in the
desert, the enemy approached with his only weapons, lies
and deceit, to attack.

*The tempter came to him and said, **"If You are
the Son of God,** tell these stones to become
bread."*

*Jesus answered, "It is written: 'Man shall not
live on bread alone, but on every word that
comes from the mouth of God.'"*

*Then the devil took him to the holy city and
had him stand on the highest point of the
temple. **"If You are the Son of God,"** he said,
"throw yourself down. For it is written: "'He
will command his angels concerning you, and
they will lift you up in their hands, so that you
will not strike your foot against a stone.'"*

*Jesus answered him, "It is also written: 'Do not
put the Lord your God to the test.'"*

*Again, the devil took him to a very high
mountain and showed him all the kingdoms of
the world and their splendor. "All this I will
give You," he said, **"if You will bow down and
worship me."***

*Jesus said to him, "Away from me, Satan! For
it is written: 'Worship the Lord your God, and
serve him only.'"*

*Then the devil left him, and angels came and
attended him.*

*Matthew 4:3-11 NIV (Author's emphasis)*

Again and again, the devil invited Jesus to forget who He
was by bringing His relationship with the Father into
question. This is the same proposition he gave Adam and
Eve, but Jesus was not swayed. We could argue that Jesus

overcame simply because He was God incarnate, but I think that misses a significant point.

Jesus refuted the temptations by knowing the character of God. He knew the map! Each temptation received a reply of Scripture. Jesus knew who He was, therefore He knew where He was. At that point of severe, physical weakness, Jesus chose to focus on the map and navigated according to the Father's unchanging nature.

"I am nourished. I will not test God. I will only worship the Lord, God."

He navigated each temptation with knowledge of the map and His location on it.

# FINDING YOUR PLACE

Throughout the Old Testament, those who did amazing things were identified by God being with them. Moses, Joshua, Caleb, all of the Judges, David, Solomon and all the rest began their amazing journeys with a common starting point: God was with them. This is important as we view life from a New Testament perspective.

Jesus brought us a much deeper understanding of what it means to have our identity rooted in God. The Son's relationship to the Father helps us to see that God being with us leads to a more intimate form of relationship. We were created to commune with God for all eternity. This is the kingdom of Heaven here and now. We are family — God's family.

The language of our key verse shows us even more.

> "I have not stopped giving thanks for you, remembering you in my prayers. I keep asking that the God of our Lord Jesus Christ, the glorious Father, may give you the Spirit of wisdom and revelation, so that you may know him better. I pray that the eyes of your heart may be enlightened in order that you may

*know the hope to which he has called you, **the riches of his glorious inheritance in his holy people,** and his incomparably great power for us who believe...."*

*Ephesians 1:16-19 NIV (Author's emphasis)*

Who receives an inheritance? An heir.

Being an heir is all about relationship, and there is one clear heir in the kingdom of God — Jesus. He is the only begotten Son (John 3:16), the only sinless man, and the Lamb sacrificed for the world (Revelation 5:6, 8). No one but Jesus has a legitimate claim to the inheritance of the Father.

Throughout His earthly ministry, Jesus did not claim an identity of His own. He always spoke of Himself in connection with the Father, only doing and saying what He saw and heard from the Father (John 5:19, 20). Everything about Jesus stemmed from His identity as the Son of God. No matter where He was physically, His constant communion with the Father meant His current location, at all times, was Heaven.

What does that mean for us? How can we possibly achieve the same thing?

We are faulty flesh, deserving of death, but Jesus Christ, the only legitimate heir, made a way for us to always find our current location. The landmarks are all over the New Testament. They go beyond His scandalous, saving grace to help us see where we are in proximity and relationship to God.

I have one request before I begin down this brief trail: Please do not pass this off as your basic Sunday School, "Jesus is the way" message and think you have heard it all before. If you truly grasp what I believe God wants you to know, your life will never be the same no matter how long you have walked with the Lord.

*Or don't you know that all of us who were baptized **into Christ Jesus** were baptized **into his** death? We were therefore buried **with him** through baptism into death in order that, just as Christ was raised from the dead through the glory of the Father, we too may live a new life. For if we have been **united with him** in a death like his, we will certainly also **be united with him** in a resurrection like his. For we know that our old self was crucified **with him** so that the body ruled by sin might be done away with, that we should no longer be slaves to sin... Now if we died **with Christ**, we believe that we will also **live with him.***

*Romans 6:3-6, 8 NIV (Author's emphasis)*

*In the same way, count yourselves dead to sin but alive to God **in Christ Jesus.***

*Romans 6:11 NIV (Author's emphasis)*

*For the wages of sin is death, but the gift of God is eternal life **in Christ Jesus** our Lord.*

*Romans 6:23 NIV (Author's emphasis)*

*Therefore, there is now no condemnation for those who are **in Christ Jesus.***

*Romans 8:1 NIV (Author's emphasis)*

Do you detect a pattern? This is a small selection, but I want to cap it with one passage in particular.

*But because of his great love for us, God, who is rich in mercy, made us alive **with Christ** even when we were dead in transgressions — it is by grace you have been saved. And God raised us up **with Christ and seated us with him** in the heavenly realms **in Christ Jesus**, in order that in the coming ages he might show the incomparable riches of his grace, expressed in his kindness to us **in Christ Jesus.***

*Ephesians 2:4-7 NIV (Author's emphasis)*

By virtue of the life, death and resurrection of Jesus Christ we can be forgiven of our sins and have eternal life in Heaven. That perspective is enough to blow your mind and set your heart free!

**And there's more....**

I speak with people all the time who are in love with Jesus and are so grateful that their eternal destiny is secure, but they do not see what has been done for them in the here and now. Somehow they think the Father is still mad at them and holding a grudge against their sin. They won't step out to do something huge, even if they feel God calling them.

I believe the biggest challenge we face is an inaccurate understanding of our current location. We get caught up in the lies the enemy whispers that cast doubts on our identities. He twists truth and tries to get us to agree with him.

It is true that we have all sinned and fallen short of the glory of God (Romans 3:23). It is true that the holy God's face is directed against sin and sinners (Psalm 34:16). **But the rest of the truth involves grace and adoption!** (Romans 8:15)

When you confess your sins and accept Jesus as Savior and Lord, you are placed **in Him.** Why does that matter? Remember proximity.

Jesus' position is that of the Son. When the Father looks at the Son, He sees everything that is right in the universe. He sees what He loves more than anything (John 17:26).

Because you are in Jesus, when the Father looks at you, He sees Jesus! Yes, you have sinned, but He doesn't see that. He sees the Lamb who was slain for all. The Father's face shines bright on you and that makes all the difference.

If you truly understand this, your life from this point forward will never be the same. If you allow yourself to believe that you are literally in Jesus, imagine what is possible! If you are at the right hand (the hand of authority) of the Father in Christ, what could ever be denied you?

If your starting point for all things and your constant, current location is the throne room of Heaven with all of the resources of the King of kings at your disposal, what could ever stop you from becoming all that is in your heart?

The Bible is the map that shows you how to navigate the all-encompassing God. Your current location is highlighted clearly now as being in Jesus and you are beginning to believe that anything is possible.

What will you set out to do? Where do you want to go? Discovering and trusting your destination is our next step.

# CHAPTER 6

# Setting Your Destination

★ ★ ★ ★ ★

*"Would you tell me, please, which way I ought to go from here?"*

*"That depends a good deal on where you want to get to," said the Cat.*

*"I don't much care where..." said Alice.*

*"Then it doesn't matter which way you go," said the Cat.*

*"...so long as I get somewhere," Alice added as an explanation.*

*"Oh, you're sure to do that," said the Cat, "if you only walk long enough."*

— *Cheshire Cat*

**Alice's Adventures In Wonderland** by Lewis Carroll

It is difficult to argue with the logic of Cheshire Cat, even if his madness is fairly obvious. The problem in this exchange lies with Alice, not the cat. I spent a ridiculous number of years asking the same kinds of questions as Alice and proved Cheshire Cat's answer true repeatedly.

Without an intentional destination, I always got somewhere, but soon I began trying to get somewhere else. After a while, my objective was more about getting away from where I was than getting to someplace I would rather be. Looking back it's easy to see why this pattern formed, and I've recognized it in many others I've coached through the years.

We are designed for **purpose** and **vision**. We crave them both! I believe the original intent of our wondrous Creator was to make us desire to turn to Him to fulfill the craving and fill us with His purposeful vision.

We'll pursue the scriptural case for this intentional design in a bit, but first, let's look at what happens when we do not turn to Him.

Since we're designed for purpose and vision, we will often accept it from the strongest influence in our lives. Purpose and vision can either come from God, or it can come from others or ourselves.

Most of us have experienced the sensation of being so caught up in something and coming down from the moment to realize we made a bad decision or were not thinking clearly about what was happening.

How is it possible that we could go along with someone or something that didn't align with who we wanted to be? Strength of influence is the key.

**Every day, with every decision, we are headed somewhere. The *where* is determined by the *why*.**

Our work is a good example of this. What you do for a career could be considered a destination. Why are you in that profession?

I speak to people weekly who do not like their jobs. They have never liked their jobs and still will not change. Most of them took their jobs because they were influenced by someone else to do so.

I have a friend who began operating heavy machinery right out of high school because it was a necessary part of his family's well-drilling and plumbing business. This decision was not based on any discernible purpose of his own other than to have income to support his young family. The strongest influences in his decision were his parents and his immediate need. Thirty years later, he is still yielding influence to his parents without setting a professional destination for himself.

Another example is a man I met who was driven to succeed. He fed his own need for purpose and vision with lofty, challenging goals, but he never considered anyone else in making them happen. Self-consumed, he wrecked a couple of marriages, lost his relationship with his children and his health suffered. Every decision came from feasting on the possessions and positions of others. Having what other people had became his burning ambition and his ultimate demise. Avoiding covetousness made the list of the Ten Commandments for multiple reasons. One of them is because it is not an effective strategy for success, health and significance. Covetousness will kill you.

In both of these examples, and many more I could cite, the strongest influence determined the destination. If we are not intentional about our influences, whatever has the most power around us becomes what we yield to. We must make conscious choices or our destinations in life will always be disappointing. They may even be destructive.

Proverbs 29:18 gives us a clear explanation of this precept. I want to break it down to the principle. This verse gives multiple perspectives depending on the translation you read.

*Where there is no vision [no redemptive
revelation of God], the people perish; but he
who keeps the law [of God, which includes that
of man] — blessed (happy, fortunate, and
enviable) is he.*

*Proverbs 29:18 AMP*

*Where there is no prophetic vision the people
cast off restraint, but blessed is he who keeps
the law.*

*Proverbs 29:18 ESV*

*If people can't see what God is doing, they
stumble all over themselves; But when they
attend to what he reveals, they are most
blessed.*

*Proverbs 29:18 MSG*

*Where there is no revelation, people cast off
restraint; but blessed is the one who heeds
wisdom's instruction.*

*Proverbs 29:18 NIV*

Each of these translations brings wisdom. I like how they round out our understanding of the principle. We are designed by God to operate and be fueled by His purposes and vision. Look at how it is described: The *"redemptive revelation of God," "prophetic vision,"* and *"see what God is doing!"*

The phrase we see as *"cast off restraint," "perish"* and *"stumble all over themselves,"* describes the result we have all experienced. This is Alice being willing to take whatever destination she gets because there is no purposeful vision to guide her.

Our final instruction gives us the key. *"Keep the law," "heed wisdom's instruction"* and *"attend to what He reveals"* in order to be *"most blessed."*

We will listen to the wise counsel of others and make our own plans (Proverbs 15:22; 16:1), but we are not sufficient in ourselves and must intentionally pursue the revelations of God as the foundation for our lives. God must be our strongest influence.

# THE PROBLEM

In Christian circles, the idea of God being the strongest influence in our lives is not very challenging on the surface. It is when we bring the idea of destination into the mix that we run across a problem. The question I most commonly hear is, "How do I know where God wants me to go?"

I'm not going to give you any specific answers as to the destinations in your life. It would be silly for me to suppose that I can say what God has in mind for you; however, I can help you tune in so that you're able to know God's will in your life better than ever before.

More often than not, having a destination in mind is not the problem we face. When we let ourselves answer the questions of destination without fear, enthusiasm and direction come forward. A clear desire begins coming from our hearts and that destination has the potential to fuel us. Fear clouds our thinking when we start wondering if the destination we want is in God's will.

This is a major battleground in spiritual warfare, one where the enemy claims countless victories. But it's time for the tide to turn and start claiming wins for God. Paul gave us our first marching order to succeed.

> *For though we live in the world, we do not wage war as the world does. The weapons we fight with are not the weapons of the world. On the contrary, they have **divine power to demolish strongholds**. We demolish arguments and every pretension that sets itself up against the knowledge of God, and **we take captive every thought to make it obedient to Christ**.*

*2 Corinthians 10:3-5 NIV (Author's emphasis)*

We have seen how satan twists scriptures to suit his schemes. One such scripture has been used as a pretense against the knowledge of God for so long that it has become a stronghold for the enemy. I am seeking to expose and destroy it right now.

> *The heart is deceitful above all things and*
> *beyond cure. Who can understand it?*
>
> *Jeremiah 17:9 NIV*

I cannot count the number of sermons and conversations I have heard with this as the central verse. The theme is always how we cannot trust our hearts and whatever desires come from it, because the heart is deceitful. There is a misbelief, perpetrated by the enemy, that our hearts are sick. Let's take that thought captive and make it obey Christ!

First, God gave us our hearts. He designed and installed them. How can we think that the God who loves us enough to come and die for our sins would equip us with such an important aspect of our existence and make it deceitful and sick? Plain and simple, this does not make sense.

The devil is not a creative being, so all he can do is pervert God's creations. Sickness and deceit are not from God, therefore, describing the heart this way is a perversion of something good. By reading the passage around the troubling verse, Jeremiah gives us the needed context to see what is actually going on.

> ***Judah's sin*** *is engraved with an iron tool,*
> *inscribed with a flint point, on the tablets of*
> ***their hearts*** *and on the horns of their altars...*
> *(vs. 1)*

> *...Through your own fault you will* ***lose the***
> ***inheritance*** *I gave you.... (vs. 4)*

> *...Cursed is the one who trusts in man, who*
> *draws strength from mere flesh and* ***whose***
> ***heart turns away from the Lord.*** *(vs. 5)*

*But blessed is the one who trusts in the Lord,
whose confidence is in him. (vs. 7)*

*The heart is deceitful above all things and
beyond cure. Who can understand it? (vs. 9)*

***I the Lord search the heart** and examine the
mind, to reward each person according to
their conduct, according to what their deeds
deserve. (vs. 10)*

*Jeremiah 17:1-10 NIV (Author's emphasis)*

Jeremiah is describing the state of affairs in the tribe of
Judah and how their sin is so deep it has scarred their
hearts. How did this happen? They put their trust in man and
turned their hearts away from the Lord.

We see clearly that a heart turned from the Lord is not
God's original intent. Since Judah repeatedly chose to turn
away from God, their sin deepened and their hearts became
sick and produced deceit.

Then in verse 10, God answered His own question of,
"Who can understand it?"

*"I the Lord search the heart..." (vs. 10)*

Through His amazing design, we see the comparison
between those who trust in man and those who trust in the
Lord.

God wouldn't search the hearts of men if they were
always deceitful and sick. **Now thanks to the amazing
work of Christ on the Cross, the hearts of those who
trust in Him have been made clean.**

God searches hearts in order to see their content and
reward each according to the conduct their content produces.
In other words, He looks past *what someone does*, to see *why
he or she did it.*

I have done some seemingly good things for selfish
reasons. There have also been times when I've messed up in

an attempt to do the right thing. God sees both and rewards each of them in kind. Throughout the Bible we see the Lord looking at the hearts of men to make a determination about them.

By making a study of the more than 700 times in Scripture in which the heart is referenced, we notice that it is not the heart itself, but the position of the heart that matters. Where is it turned and what is it receiving? This matters because the heart does not produce anything on its own. It's simply a vessel that only pours out what it receives.

Jesus emphasized this point repeatedly throughout His earthly ministry. He referred to the pure in heart (Matthew 5:8), the abundance of the heart (12:34), that which was sown in his heart (13:19) and how things we speak come from the heart (15:18). Wherever our hearts are turned our feet will follow.

How then, do we turn our hearts and make sure that the destinations flowing from them are trustworthy and within God's will?

# CHAPTER 7

# Turning with God's Presence

★ ★ ★ ★ ★

The deepest desire for any Christian is to fulfill the call of God on his or her life. We fill altars with this request and pour our desperation out at the feet of God. We often ask for a burning-bush type of moment. When we look at the only burning-bush moment recorded in history, though, we do not see Moses hearing the call and taking off after it with joy and gladness. He resisted God to His face.

This is Moses we're talking about! How could he not be ready to accept his divine calling and go after it? God gave Moses an undeniable destination, but it took some convincing, or more accurately, some *turning*.

Remember that Moses was in an identity crisis and had reinforced a new identity for himself during his years of exile. We have no record of Moses worshipping or praying to the God of his forefathers during this time. I'm not saying he was turned to wickedness, but when he encountered the burning bush, Moses' heart was not turned fully toward God.

During his experience on the far side of the wilderness, God's presence was overwhelming and Moses began to see what God was calling him to do. It is the same experience Paul prayed for the Ephesian church in our key verse.

> *I pray that the eyes of your heart may be enlightened in order that you may know the hope to which he has called you....*
>
> *Ephesians 1:18 NIV*

As Moses turned his heart toward the Lord, the call of God on his life became evident. The call of God was a destination. It's no different for you and me.

From this moment forward, Moses became the example of keeping one's heart turned toward the Lord. His life showed us what pours into the heart is what comes out. As a youth the trappings of pagan royalty and self-absorption surrounded Moses. This pours out in his response to the Egyptian beating the Israelite (Exodus 2:11-12). However, for the rest of his life (minus one hot-headed moment where he hit a rock), we see Moses pouring out the wisdom and mercy of God. The frustration and anguish of leading people whose hearts were not turned toward the Lord could have made him pack it up. Instead, Moses repeatedly interceded for them and pleaded God's own mercy back to Him.

What brought the change? At the burning bush Moses yielded his heart as a vessel for God to fill. From that day on the presence of God marked his life.

If I take my favorite coffee cup and fill it with the wonderful nectar of awareness known as coffee, what will pour out? Coffee, of course!

However, if I take that same coffee cup and fill it with rat poison, what pours out? Death. If water goes in, water comes out. If wine goes in, wine comes out. The cup does not change! It is not deceitful, wicked or sick. What goes in comes out. The vessel is an agent for what it holds. **The**

**essence and function of our hearts is to be a vessel for the presence of God.**

Only God can miraculously touch the contents of a vessel and change them. When He touches a heart it instantly pours out the things of God. The contents of Moses' heart were touched and changed at the burning bush. Similar miracles also happened to Gideon (Judges 6:11-27) and Zacchaeus (Luke 19:1-10).

A literal example happened at the wedding in Cana (John 2:1-10). Though the stone water jars were filled with water, Jesus transformed it into the richest wine through His touch.

When Jesus touches your heart, something wonderful will pour out. I have counseled people who've only had bitterness and resentment pouring in due to circumstances in their past, but as the Holy Spirit allowed me to speak the right things to them, Jesus reached in and touched what was there. In an instant, these fountains of negativity changed and their hearts turned toward God.

The enemy of God, the nemesis of man, wants to distract and draw our attention away from the things of God. But he has no real power to damage you. All he has are lies.

The devil takes God's words and tries to twist them to turn us away. For years he has taken Jeremiah 17:9 out of context to convince us that we cannot trust the desires of our hearts, but we can see overwhelming scriptural evidence that the heart gives what it receives. If I keep my heart turned toward the Lord, even when I feel dry or disconnected, the things that come from my heart will ultimately be good because the God I am pursuing is good.

My go-to verse regarding this principle is in the Psalms.

> *Take delight in the Lord, and he will give you the desires of your heart.*
>
> ***Psalm 37:4 NIV***

Would a holy and righteous God want to give us the desires of a deceitful and sick heart? Absolutely not!

The heart of a believer is not inherently bad. Your heart is good, created by a loving God to receive the goodness He will pour into it.

The Hebrew word translated as *"delight"* in Psalm 37:4 could also say, *"find yourself liking"* or *"love to be in the presence of."* When I turn my heart toward the Lord by reading and meditating on His Word, seeking Him in prayer and working to serve His children, I begin to like it and experience His presence.

The phrase translated as *"He will give"* has a double application. The translated meaning is, *"I have desires in my heart and He gives them to me."* Another application deepens the principle and gives us greater confidence. *"He will give"* is more often translated as *"He will put."* That adds an entirely new perspective!

When my heart is turned fully toward the Lord, I begin to experience His presence and He *puts* desires in my heart. The implications are huge! If I'm in His presence, the desires coming from my heart are His! By asking Him for those desires, I am not some spoiled kid trying to talk my Dad into a treat that might not be good for me. I am effectively saying, "Hey, Dad. You said it would mean a lot to You if I had this. Will You help me get it?"

As a parent, I can't imagine anything more beautiful to my ears than my kids asking me for the things I want them to have. This only happens if they stay close and spend lots of time with me. Their proximity makes me the strongest influence in their lives. The strongest influence determines where they want to go in life. How much stronger is God's influence when we are turned toward Him?

Moses ascended to leadership and grew in intimacy with the Lord due to a constant seeking and meeting with Him.

Moses even carried the "tent of meeting" as a dedicated place where he could speak with the Lord face to face (Exodus 33:7, 11).

Moses' closeness to God is well known, but I want to show you another example that seems more relatable for you and me. It happened at the same time as the miraculous transformation and journey of Moses, but it takes a little more work to piece together.

# JOSHUA, SON OF NUN

Joshua served Moses faithfully until Moses died just outside the Promised Land (Joshua 1:1). Joshua entered the scene as the chosen military leader (Exodus 17:9), and left as the one chosen to lead Israel in the successful occupation of the Promised Land (Joshua 24:31).

Why did God choose Joshua to lead the final leg of the journey? Moses was not allowed to enter the Promised Land and Joshua was merely a footnote for most of his days as the assistant. Our answer is found in those footnote moments.

Let's look at the passage about the Tent of Meeting Moses pitched outside the camp.

> *Now Moses used to take a tent and pitch it outside the camp some distance away, calling it the "tent of meeting." Anyone inquiring of the Lord would go to the tent of meeting outside the camp. And whenever Moses went out to the tent, all the people rose and stood at the entrances to their tents, watching Moses until he entered the tent. As Moses went into the tent, the pillar of cloud would come down and stay at the entrance, while the Lord spoke with Moses. Whenever the people saw the pillar of cloud standing at the entrance to the tent, they all stood and worshiped, each at the entrance to their tent. The Lord would speak to Moses face to face, as one speaks to a friend. Then Moses would return to the camp, but his*

> *young aide, Joshua son of Nun, did not leave the tent.*

*Exodus 33:7-11 NIV (Author's emphasis)*

There, in the last few words of the passage, we see something that could easily be passed over. People would come and inquire, Moses would come to meet, **but Joshua stayed and would not leave the place of God's presence.** He served Moses faithfully, but his interest was not in climbing the political ladder. **When Moses returned to camp, Joshua stayed as close to the Lord as he could.**

The vessel of Joshua's heart was open to receive all he could get from God. He believed the Lord for all the promises the nation received and trusted the desires that came from his heart. Our clearest evidence is in the account of the spies.

Each tribe chose its best man to represent them as spies in the Promised Land. Joshua was chosen from his tribe, Ephraim (Numbers 13:8). When the twelve returned, they all agreed the land was everything God promised, but ten of them were completely undone with fear because of the people who inhabited it. Instead of moving forward and believing God would give them all He had promised, their destination was a rebellion that would lead them back to slavery (14:3, 4). They were willing to go to God's presence to ask for their needs, but they had not turned their hearts. As long as their stomachs were full, they saw no need to be filled with the Lord. They let their hearts feast on fear, rumors and doubt.

Joshua and Caleb had another destination in mind. The desire of their hearts was for the place God had promised. Because they trusted the destination, they were willing to go against worldly odds in battle and stand up to their own people, even under the threat of death (Numbers 14:6-10). Joshua and Caleb had no room in their hearts for fear because they overflowed with the Lord.

Of an entire generation, Joshua and Caleb were the only two who received their inheritance in the Promised Land and their descendants were blessed because of their delight in the Lord. They trusted what came from their hearts because they trusted what poured into their hearts.

What desires and destinations come from your heart right now? If you question whether or not they are in God's will, test them — not just by the desires themselves, but by their source. What are you pouring into your heart on a regular basis?

Are you enamored by the world and what it promotes to you? What consumes the bulk of your time? Who is your life dedicated to? Do you need to get rid of some of the programs you watch, the music you listen to or the books and magazines you read? Who are your strongest influences?

Money, position and prestige are not automatic indicators of bad destinations any more than the lack of them is an indicator of holiness. Your proximity to God and the direction and content of your heart is what matters to Him.

Write your desires down and offer them to the Lord. Turn your heart fully toward Him in prayer, in seeking and in service and see what comes back. Trust the destinations that come from His presence and get ready to go after them!

We have the map. We know our location and destinations. Now let's plug in for the ultimate source of direction and guidance.

# CHAPTER 8

# **The Final Piece**

★ ★ ★ ★ ★

We lost the connection right before crossing the State Line. Our little journey back from the Quad Cities to southwest Missouri had already taken us through a hundred twists and turns, small towns and strange detours, but thanks to GPS, we were still on track.

Neither my wife nor I were familiar with the route and we ended up entirely dependent on receiving turn-by-turn instructions along the way. Approaching the Mississippi River, we noticed that the satellite icon had disappeared from the screen and the unit was guiding us based on the info from the last transmission.

Pulling into Hannibal, Missouri, we were faced with our first decision. The highway signs seemed to tell us a left turn made sense, but GPS kept us driving straight ahead. Without pulling over to consider the options, we stayed the course and kept going.

A few miles later we passed an exit with a familiar highway number on it, but GPS had us plodding on, so on we went. Twenty-five miles later, the overwhelming sense of being lost got the better of me and we stopped. Pulling up on the overpass to find a gas station, the satellite signal reconnected and a series of clicks and whirrs spun the screen and we heard, *"Recalculating."*

In a split second, our current location and desired destination were pinpointed and the perspective of the satellites rerouted us. Taking care to scan ahead on the route in case we lost connection again, we doubled back and got back on track for home.

# DECISIONS

I love using GPS, but the units we put on our dash or hold in our hands are only useful because of their satellite connection. Without the perspective that comes from being above everything, electronic maps lose context. Our locations become sketchy and our destinations become guesses.

It only took a couple of wrong decisions for Tammy and I to get completely off track. By the time we reconnected, we were miles out of the way and had to cover some of the same ground again just to get back to our original fork in the road.

Life is one fork in the road after another. At each intersection we have to make a decision. Each decision leads us to another. If we're doing things in a kingdom-minded way, each decision brings us more in alignment with God. But even when we're moving within God's will, there are still choices that must be made.

Some of the decisions are easier and we can make them based on our own familiarity with the map and knowledge of the area. Others require more than we possess. In the natural world this is where the guidance of satellites comes in, but when we look at the journey toward authentic manhood, our only hope for real guidance is the Holy Spirit.

This becomes a sensitive area for many men I speak with who have a lot of biblical knowledge — not that they discount the guidance of Holy Spirit, but because they have a lot of confidence in their own knowledge of the Scriptures.

We would do well to remember that knowledge of a map is not the same thing as having a guide who knows every inch and nuance of the land. Knowing the words in the Bible is not the same as having the Spirit of God make it come alive and reveal its infinite depth and truth.

The Pharisees were extremely knowledgeable of Scripture, yet Jesus pointed out that their knowledge was not the answer to what they were seeking.

> *You study the Scriptures diligently because*
> *you think that in them you have eternal life.*
> *These are the very Scriptures that testify about*
> *me, yet you refuse to come to me to have life.*
>
> *John 5:39, 40 NIV*

The devil knows the Bible. This is evidenced by his ability to misuse its words. He served around the throne of God before his rebellion and fall. He is familiar with the terrain we are discussing but he refused to make the right decisions.

Paul had an intimate understanding of this principle. He was educated as a Pharisee and that led him to persecute the Early Church (Philippians 3:5, 6). But after his conversion to follow Jesus, we see a new understanding of the same scriptures flowing from him. Our key verses reveal why.

> *I have not stopped giving thanks for you,*
> *remembering you in my prayers. I keep asking*
> *that the God of our Lord Jesus Christ, the*
> *glorious Father, may **give you the Spirit of***
> ***wisdom and revelation**, so that you may know*
> *him better....*
>
> *Ephesians 1:16-19 NIV (Author's emphasis)*

*For this reason, since the day we heard about you, we have not stopped praying for you. We continually ask God to fill you with the knowledge of His will **through all the wisdom and understanding that the Spirit gives**...*

*Colossians 1:9-11 NIV (Author's emphasis)*

The most compelling example of what Jesus spoke to the Pharisees about, Paul knows exactly what we need. Revelation is what turns knowledge into wisdom and revelation is the realm of Holy Spirit.

The word "revelation" means something is revealed, not created. That means the thing revealed is already there. But if it's already there, why does it require the Holy Spirit for us to connect and see it? Paul tells us.

*We do, however, speak a message of wisdom among the mature, but not the wisdom of this age or of the rulers of this age, who are coming to nothing. No, we declare God's wisdom, **a mystery that has been hidden and that God destined for our glory before time began.***

*1 Corinthians 2:6, 7 NIV (Author's emphasis)*

Solomon, the wisest man ever known, also addresses this interaction with God that takes place, saying, *"It is the glory of God to conceal a matter; to search out a matter is the glory of kings"* (Proverbs 25:2 NIV).

In the Old Testament and New, God has told us repeatedly that there are things hidden for us to find.

*I will give you hidden treasures, riches stored in secret places, so that you may know that I am the LORD, the God of Israel, who summons you by name.*

*Isaiah 45:3 NIV*

*So was fulfilled what was spoken through the prophet: "I will open my mouth in parables, I*

*will utter things hidden since the creation of
the world."*

*Matthew 13:35 NIV*

*Where then does wisdom come from? Where
does understanding dwell? It is hidden from
the eyes of every living thing, concealed even
from the birds in the sky.*

*Job 28:20, 21 NIV*

*For whatever is hidden is meant to be
disclosed, and whatever is concealed is meant
to be brought out into the open.*

*Mark 4:22 NIV*

This divine game of hide-and-seek is the single biggest
difference we can see between those favored by God and
those who are ultimately condemned. In order to live with a
heart fully turned toward God, we must be seeking Him, His
wisdom and His ways. Our earthly preoccupation should be
to seek the things He has hidden for us.

The previous passage from Paul in 1 Corinthians 2 paints
the best picture of the relationship between God's favor,
seeking His wisdom and the Holy Spirit's role in making it all
happen.

> *We do, however, speak a message of wisdom
> among the mature, but not the wisdom of this
> age or of the rulers of this age, who are
> coming to nothing. No, we declare God's
> wisdom, a mystery that has been hidden and
> that God destined for our glory before time
> began. **None of the rulers of this age
> understood it,** for if they had, they would not
> have crucified the Lord of glory. However, as
> it is written: What no eye has seen, what no
> ear has heard, and what no human mind has
> conceived — **the things God has prepared for
> those who love him** — these are the things
> **God has revealed to us by his Spirit. The
> Spirit searches all things,** even the deep
> things of God. For who knows a person's
> thoughts except their own spirit within them?*

> *In the same way **no one knows the thoughts of God except the Spirit of God.** What we have received is not the spirit of the world, but **the Spirit who is from God,** so that we may understand what God has freely given us. This is what we speak, not in words taught us by human wisdom but in words **taught by the Spirit,** explaining spiritual realities with Spirit-taught words. **The person without the Spirit does not accept the things that come from the Spirit of God but considers them foolishness, and cannot understand them because they are discerned only through the Spirit.***

*1 Corinthians 2:6-14 NIV (Author's emphasis)*

Worldly knowledge and human wisdom is what we can attain on our own and is limited by our flesh. Even the divinely inspired words of the Bible are human words, the same as any other book. They have been read and taught for centuries to people and by people who obviously did not understand. The words are not the key.

God has hidden infinite layers of His thoughts within the words He inspired. No one knows those thoughts better than the Spirit of God, and **we have received the Spirit!** Get this locked into your being!

- Our eternal lives, as well as our daily walk as men of God, hinges on our ability to discern and follow His will.

- To know His will and make sense of decisions we must make every day, we must have His wisdom.

- His wisdom has been hidden for us to find as we seek Him; however, we won't understand it on our own because His ways are so much higher than ours (Isaiah 55:9).

- In order to understand the will and wisdom of God, we need the Spirit of God.

- By accepting and following Jesus as your Lord and Savior, you receive the Holy Spirit!

This revelation is almost too much to take in on its own. We can receive the same Spirit who descended from Heaven and guided Jesus throughout His earthly ministry! Receiving the Holy Spirit was so important to Jesus that He began preparing the disciples for it before His crucifixion.

> *If you love me, keep my commands. And I will ask the Father, and he will give you another advocate **to help you and be with you forever — the Spirit of truth.** The world cannot accept him, because it neither sees him nor knows him. But you know him, for he lives with you and will be in you.*

> *John 14:15-17 NIV  (Author's emphasis)*

> *All this I have spoken while still with you. But the Advocate, **the Holy Spirit,** whom the Father will send in my name, **will teach you all things and will remind you of everything I have said to you.***

> *John 14:25, 26 NIV  (Author's emphasis)*

The disciples had serious concerns about being without Jesus and being on their own. They had learned so much up until that point, but how would they learn more about the kingdom if their Teacher were gone? Where would their guidance come from if Jesus were not there in the flesh to tell them where to go?

Their questions about guidance then are the same as ours today. Jesus' answer to them is His answer to us as we complete our *Manhood GPS.*

# CHAPTER 9

# The Spirit Completes
# Your GPS

★ ★ ★ ★ ★

*But very truly I tell you, it is for your good
that I am going away. Unless I go away, the
Advocate will not come to you; but if I go, I
will send Him to you.*

*John 16:7 NIV*

How could it be? After three years of studying at His feet,
seeing and participating in extreme miracles and believing
that He was the promised Messiah, Jesus told His closest
friends He was going away.

Can you imagine their dismay? The very One who was
the embodiment of all they had hoped for was leaving. How
heartbroken and confused they must have felt.

To make it even more troublesome, Jesus told them it was
actually good that He was going away! The same Greek
word, *"sumphero,"* translated as *"good"* in the NIV is more
often translated as *"expedient"* or *"profitable"* in other
translations. For me, using *"expedient"* brings greater clarity

to their situation and ours while giving insight to Jesus' point of view.

*"Expedient,"* as an adjective, describes *"something that gives an advantage or promotes a desired objective under the current circumstances."* So if it was expedient for Jesus to leave and Holy Spirit to come, what was the objective the disciples had been given? Look back a few pages in the Bible to see where everything came together.

In John 15, Jesus shared the analogy of the Vine and branches for the express purpose of giving His disciples their objective: Bearing fruit that lasts (vs. 16).

What is the fruit that lasts? Love.

This is one of the places I feel the enemy has gained the most ground against men throughout the centuries. By distorting and perverting the concept of love, satan has tricked us into agreeing with an exclusively emotional and disposable kind of love — the kind of love that comes from hormones and is easily discarded when the feeling wears off. This is not the kind of love that comes from God.

Real love is an action, not a feeling. It involves choice and dedication. The love Jesus exemplified and passed on to us is the most masculine thing in existence. We must reclaim it if we are to find our way as men. Jesus wanted His disciples to understand this concept.

## THE VINEYARD

Systematically, Jesus explained what His disciples must do and how they must do it in the context of a vineyard. I personally believe they were beside or passing through a vineyard when this lesson took place.

By touching the vine and the branches and pointing out the vinedresser as he worked, Jesus was able to give His disciples an understanding of how the love of the Father passed through Him to them. The natural result of a healthy branch receiving nutrients from the vine and care from the vinedresser is fruit.

In verse 9, Jesus transitions from grapes, a fruit that passes away, to the fruit that remains — love.

> *As the Father has loved (cared for and nourished) me, so have I loved (cared for and nourished) you. Now remain in my love.*
>
> *John 15:9 NIV (Author's paraphrase)*

The natural question that would follow, at least for me, would be: **How do I remain in Your love?** After all, we were told in verses 2 and 6 it's possible to be pruned from the vine and rendered useless. But I want to remain! I'm so thankful Jesus knew I would ask.

> *If you keep My commands, you will remain in my love, just as I have kept my Father's commands and remain in his love.*
>
> *John 15:10 NIV*

As always, Jesus leads by example and completes the analogy when He gives us His command: *"Love each other as I have loved you"* (vs. 12).

The Vine is love. The Vinedresser is love. The nourishment provided by being in the Vine is love. We remain in the Vine by love. The fruit we produce as a result is love. **Love is our ultimate location, destination and guide.** So why did Jesus flank this discourse on love with the promise of the Holy Spirit? (See John 14:15-26; 15:26–16:15.)

If the Beatles were right and "all we need is love," why was it better for Jesus to leave and for the Holy Spirit to come? Because we do not currently live in the protected confines of God's vineyard. Remember our definition of the word "expedient" was about promoting a desired objective (fruit that remains, love) **under current circumstances.**

Immediately after the vineyard analogy on love, Jesus shows the disciples the current circumstances.

> *If the world hates you, keep in mind that it hated me first. If you belonged to the world, it would love you as its own.* **As it is, you do not belong to the world, but I have chosen you out of the world.** **That is why the world hates you.**

> *John 15:18, 19 NIV (Author's emphasis)*

Jesus says, point blank, "If you love as I love, you will be hated." The disciples had seen the resistance and examples of hatred while walking with Jesus, but they had not taken it to heart yet. They were with Jesus and He had handled everything up until this point. There was no ownership of the love they must begin to carry.

As long as Jesus remained on Earth, the disciples would defer to Him and never have the fullness of faith on their own. The adversity they encountered would be too much for them if they were always looking to Jesus for a bailout. And so, Jesus tells them, "It is expedient (good) for you that I go away."

For three chapters and in multiple locations, Jesus tells them about the Holy Spirit and why His coming matters to them. The Holy Spirit would remind them of what Jesus had said (14:26) and guide them into all things (16:13) because Jesus did not want them to fall away (16:1) and so they could have peace (16:33).

When the whole world is set against your objective and destination, the obstacles are unimaginable. At each roadblock, a decision must be made to determine which direction to go and your entire journey can hang in the balance. Jesus not only knew, but He told the disciples they would face hate, exclusion and death for His name.

The Lord knew the strength they would need to make the right decisions and how weak each of them were at that time. The disciples needed a difference maker of Heavenly proportion.

# THE DIFFERENCE OF THE SPIRIT

Peter is an easy target for a lot of sermons that allow us mere mortals to relate to someone with larger-than-life significance. His impulsive, hotheaded and cowardly actions prior to Jesus' resurrection are a stark contrast to the bold, confident leader of the Church we see on and after Pentecost.

On the night of Jesus' arrest, Peter went from being the guy who drew his sword to defend the Lord to the guy who denied Him three times while hiding in the shadows as Jesus was tried and beaten (John 18:10, 15-26). He was not exactly building a great résumé as an Early-Church father.

But Jesus had seen more in him than Peter himself knew was there. Calling him "the rock" long before Peter showed any sign of being stable (Matthew 16:17, 18), Jesus prophesied that Peter would be the man who would rise once he received the power of the Holy Spirit.

Everything changed for Peter and everyone else in the upper room at Pentecost. Jesus ascended to the right hand of the Father and the Father began pouring out His Holy Spirit. The same Peter, who shrunk in fear and lied to a little girl when confronted about Jesus, stood in front of thousands and proclaimed Jesus' name and righteousness (Acts 2:14-41).

For the remainder of his life, Peter made decisions with the Holy Spirit's power. He entered the house of Cornelius, a Gentile, which was strictly forbidden to a Jew (Acts 10). Along with John, Peter chose to be beaten rather than to deny Christ. The account of Peter and John before the Sanhedrin shows us that others also noticed the difference in Peter.

> *When they saw the courage of Peter and John*
> *and realized that they were unschooled,*

> *ordinary men, they were astonished and they*
> *took note that these men had been with Jesus.*

> *Acts 4:13 NIV*

The phrase *"unschooled, ordinary men"* is a key. Peter had just given the religious academics a clear, educated and articulate answer through the power of the Holy Spirit despite his absolute lack of qualification to give such an answer.

The Greek word translated *"ordinary men"* in Acts 4:13 is *"idiotes,"* which is where we get our word, *"idiots."* The Sanhedrin were astonished by the answers because they believed Peter and John were idiots. The only thing to which they could attribute the wisdom of these Apostles was their proximity to Jesus.

We know that Peter was filled with the Holy Spirit, but all the people around them saw was Jesus. That's exactly what Jesus said the Holy Spirit would do.

> *But when he, the Spirit of truth, comes, he will*
> *guide you into all the truth. He will not speak*
> *on his own; he will speak only what he hears,*
> *and he will tell you what is yet to come. **He***
> ***will glorify me** because it is from me that he*
> *will receive what he will make known to you.*

> *John 16:13,14 NIV (Author's emphasis)*

The disciples learned by losing the external, physical presence of Jesus, they gained His internal presence. All of the wisdom, love and companionship they had grown accustomed to when they gathered around the Lord was now with them always, no matter where they were.

By receiving the Holy Spirit, they had Jesus in multiplied form. Instead of working *with* them, He began to work *through* them. This is the exact same offer made to each of us.

You cannot walk with a physical, flesh-and-blood Jesus right now but it wasn't until He left that the disciples truly became world changers. They founded the Church amidst great controversy and became known as the men who turned the world upside-down! (Acts 17:6 ESV) All by the power of the Holy Spirit.

Very few of us are likely to face anything similar to the Early Church because our enemies are dressed differently. The arguments against God are more subtle and less abrasive, but make no mistake; the cause of Christ is being opposed in your own home, work and community through powerful influences. Our need for the Holy Spirit to guide our decisions on a moment-to-moment basis is dire and cannot be ignored.

Jesus knew we would need the Holy Spirit. He said we only needed to ask for Him and the Father would gladly give Him (Luke 11:13). Let's look at how we can access this greatest of all Guides in order to make decisions and choose our path for the kingdom's sake.

# CHAPTER 10

# Hearing the Holy Spirit

★ ★ ★ ★ ★

My son was getting frustrated. I had only been watching for a few minutes, but I knew what needed to happen. He was playing a video game centered on problem solving and this particular level had him stumped.

After witnessing a few failed attempts, I offered some advice but he completely ignored it and met his virtual doom once again. Thinking he must not have heard me, I knelt down by his chair and started to tell him again.

"I don't want help, please," he barked, "I want to do it on my own!"

Just before I could be offended, the Holy Spirit got ahold of me. "That's exactly how you've acted toward Me countless times. Now you have some perspective."

Ouch.

I've worked with thousands of people in long- and short-term capacities as a coach or consultant and heard them all say, "I really want to hear God's guidance but He just isn't speaking to me." For a long time I took what they said at face value until the realization hit me that this is seldom true.

# INTERFERENCE

Too many of us don't hear clearly from the Holy Spirit and think it's a trouble with transmission, the way the satellites are not sending good signals to my car. But if you've used GPS for very long, you know as well as I do there are things that can get in the way or hinder our ability to receive the signals.

God will guide us. He is speaking. Let's look at two of many verses that assure us of God's desire to guide.

> *He guides the humble in what is right and teaches them his way.*
>
> *Psalm 25:9 NIV*

> *I will instruct you and teach you in the way you should go; I will counsel you with my loving eye on you.*
>
> *Psalm 32:8 NIV*

As our Father, He wants to be involved in our lives and see us succeed. He will guide us. Similar to our earthly GPS, though, things can prevent our communication. Let's make sure our channels are clear.

When I pray with people in the altars at churches, camps or conferences, I often ask them if there is anything between their heart and God's (anything they need to confess and make right before we begin to ask for what they need). I'm asking you that question right now.

**Is there anything in the way that would prevent you from hearing the Holy Spirit's voice?**

It may not be dramatic but it could still be blocking your reception. Perhaps there's a lingering issue that needs to be laid down. Ask the Holy Spirit to reveal to you anything in the way and be ready to respond.

> **Sin** — Sin is obviously on the list of possible blockages. One of the primary functions of the Holy Spirit is the conviction of sin (John 16:8) and in many testimonies, this is the first time people acknowledge hearing from God. They're convinced of the sin in their lives and respond to the offer of salvation. But a one-time experience doesn't mean it's all gone. Is there something being brought to your mind right now? If so, please deal with it.

> **Shame** — On the other side of the sin coin is the oldest form of interference: Shame. When Adam and Eve heard God in the Garden after their disobedience, they hid because of shame (Genesis 3:7-10).

> Realization of our sin is supposed to bring humility and repentance, not shame. Jesus did not offer us shame in exchange for our sin, but freedom. Lay shame down and walk away from it as a son of God.

> **Pride** — Sometimes we are proud and want to solve things on our own. That might work with a video game, but navigating the pitfalls and opportunities of life has much higher stakes. We are not told to be humble because God wants us low, but because He cares for us. Real humility is to place ourselves under His mighty hand so that He can lift us up (1 Peter 5:6-7).

> **Stubbornness** — There are also times when we seek guidance but are actually hoping for reinforcement for the decision we've already made. If I can say, "God told me to," it changes everything and removes the responsibility from me. Jesus addressed this during the Sermon on the Mount.

*Not everyone who says to me, 'Lord, Lord,' will enter the kingdom of heaven, but only the one who does the will of my Father who is in heaven.*

*Matthew 7:21 NIV*

Just using Jesus' name or invoking God over what you're doing doesn't make it His will. The idea of being living sacrifices (Romans 12:1) means we're intentionally subject to His instruction. This is a choice, not some robotic response to salvation. Jesus said, *"Anyone who **chooses** to do the will of God..."* (John 7:17), so we must consciously declare that we choose His will.

By choosing Him and His will, we enter into relationship with Jesus and become part of the Vine.

Too many people think of their relationship with God only as a Master-servant arrangement and never move into the depths that Jesus offered. Jesus gives us another aspect of our obedience to His command of love.

*"**You are My friends if you do what I command.** I no longer call you servants, because a servant does not know his master's business. Instead, I have called you friends, for everything that I learned from My Father I have made known to you."*

***John 15:14, 15 NIV (Author's emphasis)***

**The God of all things offers us His friendship and wants to tell us all things.** Our motivation for obedience in any situation is gratitude and love. He gave it all to save us and to have us in close, personal relationship with Him. How can we not want to be closer and know Him more?

As we draw closer to Him, we become better able to receive His guidance. When nothing is in the way and we're gaining stronger connection, our true nature of being able to easily commune with God is revealed. We're now ready to receive.

# METHODS OF COMMUNICATION

In listening for God's guidance, the first principle we must observe is following what is already revealed. If I am praying my heart out about something, but ignoring or not seeking what is easily offered to me in Scripture, I will probably be frustrated.

Paul wrote to Timothy, *"All Scripture is God-breathed and is useful for teaching, rebuking, correcting and training in righteousness, so that the servant of God may be thoroughly equipped for every good work"* (2 Timothy 3:16, 17 NIV). I like the idea of being thoroughly equipped! According to Paul, that happens through Scripture.

What we find in reading the Bible for guidance is a lot of general instructions with which to begin. We read about relationships and how to treat others, our relationship with God Himself and how to grow with Him and about relationships with our parents, siblings, neighbors, friends, bosses, employees, authority figures, spouses and other believers to name a few.

The Bible speaks of character and moral absolutes as well as our attitudes toward material possessions and the treatment of our gifts and talents. There are precepts about sexual thoughts and actions alongside wisdom regarding how we use our words. Much of God's will has already been made plain in the Bible and it really does cover everything.

Some of the things you may not find are the *specifics* of how they apply directly to your life. You are told what kind of husband to be, and even the kind of woman to marry, but not specifically who that woman should be.

Guidance on the kind of employee you should be is found, but nothing on whether or not you should take that promotion, change jobs or start your own business. God may use a specific sign to guide on a specific issue, but more often than not we are expected to make decisions based on what we know about Him.

If we're making a sincere effort to follow and implement the guidance God has clearly laid out in Scripture, we can have confidence He will give us the specific help we need when the time is right. We're to handle what we have and believe the rest is coming.

Faith is an essential part of the Holy Spirit's guidance. Remember, He is within us and is often His voice is blended in with ours. That's not necessarily a bad thing.

# UNCONSCIOUS GUIDANCE

When our hearts are turned toward God, He is what is pouring in and we are becoming what He wants us to be — more like Jesus.

By pressing in deeper to who Jesus is and spending time in reading and prayer, under the Holy Spirit's influence, we develop a sense of how Jesus thinks. This is what Paul meant by *"the mind of Christ"* (1 Corinthians 2:16, Philippians 2:5). Just as we do many things unconsciously because we're so used to doing them, God's guidance can flow through us even when we're unaware it's Him.

The more time you spend intentionally engaged with the Holy Spirit, the more you'll operate under His guidance without even realizing it. We must have faith this is happening. Solomon spoke of this.

> *Trust in the Lord with all your heart and lean not on your own understanding; in all your ways submit to him, and he will make your paths straight."*
>
> *Proverbs 3:5-6 NIV*

This is a promise! If we trust with all our heart and lean on Him, He will guide us. It doesn't say we'll always be aware He is guiding us, just that He will. We follow His clearly revealed lead with right hearts and He lays out the path and helps us walk it. But we must be the ones walking.

I love that Moses was being sent by God through a miraculous sign to achieve a miraculous deliverance of Israel and still being expected to walk it all out in faith. When Moses asked, *"Who am I?"* God answered, *"I will be with you,"* and then God offered him a sign.

> *...And this will be the sign to you that it is I who have sent you: When you have brought the people out of Egypt, you will worship God on this mountain.*
>
> *Exodus 3:12 NIV*

In other words, **Moses was to know that God was with him AFTER everything was accomplished!** Most of us want confirmation long before we take our first step, but God puts it to us differently. "Walk in faith that I'm with you. You probably won't know for sure until you look back and see Me throughout it all."

With the benefit of history, we can see that Moses could have been totally assured from the beginning, but in the moment, God wanted him to have faith. There is more glory and pleasure for God when we trust Him.

> *Without faith, it is impossible to please God.*
>
> *Hebrews 11:6 NIV*

As a father, I love it when my kids simply do what I tell them and trust me that it will work out, knowing that I have their best interests at heart. Their love, admiration and respect for me go up when that happens as well. We are all elevated and we grow closer together.

When we attend to our duty of pursuing God, His guidance in our lives is a natural result. We can trust Him to be faithful in His promise of guidance, even if we don't recognize His handiwork in the moment and can only appreciate it afterward.

In every instance it's important for us to follow the general guidance, but it's not our only means of receiving. We need the Lord's guidance for specific issues, too. Though I can't tell you what that advice will be, there are guidelines to help us discern the way He would have us go.

# CHAPTER 11

# Guardrails for Specific Guidance

★ ★ ★ ★ ★

God's means of guidance in the Bible are varied, but they track right along with what people experience today. Dreams, visions and the audible voice of God are still part of the Christian life, though only a small percentage of believers seem to experience guidance this way. A larger percentage of people, myself included, more consistently experience the Lord's guidance through the internal or "still, small voice" and the promptings of the Holy Spirit.

Two other types of guidance that are often overlooked or undervalued have also meant a lot to me: The advice of others and discerning from circumstances.

By drawing nearer to the Holy Spirit, you will begin to sense Him in these different ways. It is likely that you will have certain ways you realize His presence more readily than others. In whatever way that is, embrace it!

Ever since I was very young, God has spoken to me through other people, though I didn't realize it was the Holy Spirit at the time. One person God used in particular to speak to me is my Grandma Anita. For my entire life, she has been the most consistent one to speak hard truth when no one else would and to give me just the right encouragement when I was in need.

When I began to realize how God spoke to me through others, I instantly nicknamed Grandma, "The Voice of God." Her words are still major guiding points for me.

Another key way I hear from God is by journaling. Not in a "Dear Diary" sort of way, but as a means of capturing my thoughts. The still, small voice of the Holy Spirit is too easy for me to pass by in the heat of my day. But when I sit down and write my thoughts out and pray through my pen, I slow down and listen better. And since I'm already writing, I can record the impressions and words I receive. Keeping track of what we hear and how we hear it helps us to build our personal history with God and we learn to know Him better as a result.

I have good friends who receive guidance regularly through dreams, but I can only recall a few of those times myself. Others I know have incredibly detailed and accurate visions, which I think would be very cool, but so far, that's never happened to me. The audible voice of God? Not me. At least, not yet.

## SCRIPTURAL BACKING

Regardless of how you receive it, guidance must check out in terms of being from God. This is a spiritual matter and there are spiritual forces at work in this world seeking to distract and deceive you.

> *For our struggle is not against flesh and blood,*
> *but against the rulers, against the authorities,*
> *against the powers of this dark world and*

*against the spiritual forces of evil in the heavenly realms.*

*Ephesians 6:12 NIV*

We must be vigilant, though not afraid, in ensuring our guidance is pure. From our own selfishness and the deceit of the enemy, we must guard our hearts. That's why we must have guidelines to help us along.

I remember speaking with a man who asked for counsel about some major life changes. When he first started talking I got a "check" in my spirit. He was a nice enough guy and said all the right Christian words, but I just knew there was something that didn't line up in the story he told about some of his actions and the faith he claimed.

"I was really torn about it for a long time," he started, "but after a lot of prayer and seeking the Lord, it was obvious God was telling me to leave my wife and start over."

It took me a second to get my head around what he was saying. After asking a few basic biblical questions regarding his marriage, it was obvious this supposed leading was not from the God of the Bible. I did not make that determination based on some amazing spiritual insight, but by some simple, reliable rules for discerning God's leading.

When we receive guidance on a specific issue by one of the means discussed previously, we still need to check it out.

The man claimed to have a strong internal witness from the Holy Spirit and multiple dreams that led him to this conclusion. When I asked him where he found the scriptural backing for the decision, he said, "Oh, I didn't get it from the Bible. It was purely the Holy Spirit."

This is a principle we can be very clear about: **God, Jesus and the Holy Spirit are all in alignment with each other and their guidance will always be in alignment with the Bible.** No exceptions!

Countless people have taken a small passage or verse and manipulated it to say what they wanted, ignoring both context and meaning, but that doesn't make them led by God. This is another reason that personal, intimate knowledge of the Word of God is so important. **The Holy Spirit will never give guidance contrary to the revealed guidance of the Bible, which He inspired in the first place.**

# PEACE OF MIND

Jesus left His peace with us so our hearts would not be troubled (John 14:27). Paul instructed us to *"Let the peace of Christ rule in your hearts"* (Colossians 3:15 NIV). Our personal peace is a big deal to God. It's a primary weapon of our warfare.

In decision-making, our peace of mind is a great indicator regarding any situation we face. The word translated *"rule"* in Colossians 3:15, has the implication of *"judging or deciding for the awarding of prizes."* Is the peace of Christ my ruling influence? Do I have peace about the thing I want to have or feel led to do?

Peace of mind is important in those corridor moments when we approach a closed door. Maybe God will open it. Maybe He won't. But if I feel strongly that He wants me to go through that door, I need to have a peace that He will open it and not force myself through.

But if I am not sure God wants me in that door, I should wait. A lack of peace is strong guidance and it can save us a lot of trouble if we'll only yield to its wisdom.

# CIRCUMSTANCES

Part of our Christian responsibility in this life is to maintain an awareness of our surroundings. We need to pay attention and know what is happening around us. Through the help of the Holy Spirit, we can also see beyond what is stirring on the surface of issues to discern underlying factors.

Similar to the unopened door, we must open our hearts and consider if God is speaking to us and guiding by the circumstances surrounding our decisions. Just as when Grandpa Howard would follow the most obvious route to a house, only to find the river swelled to twice its size and blocking the way, different circumstances often require a different approach.

It's important that we also realize the difference between *considering* circumstances and *allowing them to take control*. A life in Christ will often call us to face the circumstances and tell them to bow a knee to Christ in us. Circumstances do not rule, but they can be useful guardrails as we seek guidance.

# WORDS FROM OTHERS

*Plans fail for lack of counsel, but with many advisers they succeed.*

*Proverbs 15:22 NIV*

We are meant to have brothers in Christ surrounding us, pouring into our lives and us pouring into them. Most of my life up into my thirties was spent walking a little bit apart and I had no dedicated, godly men to lean on.

This is not to exclude women in the role of bringing words from God. I already told you how my Grandma Anita and my mom have been instrumental in this role. The Holy Spirit uses my wife to give me perspective I would have ignored otherwise and there are other women I know and respect that God has used in guiding me. However, iron sharpens iron (Proverbs 27:17), and this is the role of strong, godly men in your life.

The closeness and bond I share with the strong men in my life now is worth much more than gold. I know they are seeking the Lord personally and they know that I am. We seek each other's counsel and discuss revelation as well as help with decisions.

It is these kinds of relationships that are not only useful in making great decisions, but they are life giving. If you don't have these kinds of people in your life, you need them. If you don't have strong men to speak into your life, contact me through the info in the back of this book and I will help you connect with a **FivestarMan** group. It's that important.

Please note that all the guidelines and methods of guidance we have covered do not normally stand alone. The Holy Spirit is masterful at weaving multiple ways of communication together in order to reach us.

In my life He has given me a dream, followed by a confirming word from someone, impressed me with an answer and then confirmed it with circumstances. All that for one piece of guidance. He has also given me simple, quiet and peaceful assurance that I am on the right track and need only to keep going and remain faithful.

How He guides is His business. I'm certainly not in a position to tell Him how it should be done. My jobs were outlined in an old hymn years ago: "Trust and obey." Once I realize that He is guiding me, the rest is execution on my part.

Finally, in terms of guidelines that assist us in receiving and discerning God's guidance, Henry Drummond, a well-known author of the 19th century who assisted D.L. Moody in his evangelistic campaigns, wrote on the flyleaf of his Bible a concise summary for seeking the will and guidance of God. I now write it inside the cover of new journals for reference:

1. *Pray.*

2. *Think.*

3.  *Talk to wise people; but do not regard their decision as final.*

4.  *Beware of the bias of your own will; but do not be too much afraid of it. (God never unnecessarily thwarts a man's nature and likings, and it is a mistake to think that His will is in the line of the disagreeable.)*

5.  *Meantime do the next thing (for doing God's will in small things is the best preparation for knowing it in the great things).*

6.  *When decision and action are necessary, go ahead.*

7.  *Never reconsider the decision when it is finally acted upon.*

8.  *You will probably not find out till afterwards, perhaps long afterwards, that you have been led at all.*

**Though not always easy, we can rest assured, God wants to guide us.**

One question that has come up in my life and I've been asked numerous times by others is what I do when it seems God has stopped guiding. Maybe I was hearing Him loud and clear for a while, but now... not so much. I have had an exciting and comforting revelation brought to me about this dilemma.

That's next.

# CHAPTER 12

# The Road to Maturity

★ ★ ★ ★ ★

There's a stark difference between knowing who Jesus is and actually accepting Him as your Lord. My entire life, it seems I've known Jesus and believed Him to be the Son of God, but I did not actually give Him my life and proclaim His lordship until well into adulthood.

Though not a new convert in the strictest sense, my experience was totally new to me. I began feeling, hearing and seeing the Holy Spirit work in amazing ways. Prophetic insight when dealing with people came fast and strong. I saw cancer removed, limbs grown and people restored with prayer as well as receiving an unexpected flow of wisdom and knowledge while teaching.

Something else got my attention right away. The guidance of God was loud, clear and frequent. It was like wearing an earpiece and microphone wired to the throne room of Heaven. Honestly it felt very easy for a while.

Everywhere I looked, the Holy Spirit was bringing obvious communication to me and I started thinking it would always be that way.

It wouldn't.

Not that the guidance disappeared, but it wasn't as easy to discern. I sought advice and learned how to check for interference, but my channels were clear. For the first time in my life, I was seriously on fire for Jesus. I loved learning and had my heart turned to Him. So why the difficulty?

I drew some help out of a comment I read from Hudson Taylor, founder of the China Inland Mission and a giant in the faith. His story is incredibly inspirational. He was someone I figured who had very easily heard from God, but he gave me an insight I didn't expect.

As a young Christian, Taylor had something similar to my experience and said the Lord guided and directed him in very specific ways. Later on, as he matured in his faith and was eventually responsible for thousands of missionaries, Taylor commented, "Now as I have gone on, and God has used me more and more, I seem often to be like a man going along in a fog. I do not know what to do."

How could that be?

Paul speaks to this issue in his writings when illuminates the different stages of spiritual growth.

> *Brothers and sisters, I could not address you as people who live by the Spirit but as people who are still worldly — **mere infants in Christ.***
>
> *1 Corinthians 3:1 NIV (Author's emphasis)*
>
> *When I was a child, I talked like a child, I thought like a child, I reasoned like a child. When I became a man, **I put the ways of childhood behind me.***
>
> *1 Corinthians 13:11 NIV (Author's emphasis)*

*"Until we all reach unity in the faith and in the knowledge of the Son of God and **become mature,** attaining to the whole measure of the fullness of Christ. Then **we will no longer be infants,** tossed back and forth by the waves, and blown here and there by every wind of teaching and by the cunning and craftiness of people in their deceitful scheming.*

*Ephesians 4:13, 14 NIV (Author's emphasis)*

**Therefore let us move beyond the elementary teachings** *about Christ and* **be taken forward to maturity...**

*Hebrews 6:1 NIV (Author's emphasis)*

Inherent in Paul's comments is an understanding that our growth in spirit is progressive, like our physical growth. An infant has different needs than a teenager and the teen's needs are different than an adult male's. The needs of nourishment and health are basically the same, but how it is accomplished is very different.

As new Christians, we are babes and require much more care and attention. Paul uses the analogy of milk versus meat in 1 Corinthians 3 and Hebrews 5. Early we are fed what we can handle and will result in our health and growth, but with growth comes increasing responsibility to do more for ourselves. We are weaned from complete dependence so we can mature.

This doesn't mean we're going out on our own and away from God's wisdom and power. God forbid! It simply means that the expectation is for us to learn and be able to make more decisions on our own because of what we know about our Father. He equipped us with our intellects and He certainly doesn't want us to forsake our intelligence at conversion. He wants our minds turned over to His glory.

So the remarkable and easily accessible guidance I received in my early walk gave way to my own deepening knowledge of God. There are things He expects me to know

to build a more substantial faith. When my son was a baby, I
had to tell him not to chew on knives and protect him from
the blades because he didn't understand the danger. Now he
has full access to an entire collection of knives and we
discuss their care, use and craftsmanship. I never have to tell
him those things from his infancy again because I expect him
to know.

Whether communicating with the Holy Spirit is new to
you or you've done it for years, don't expect it to always be
the same. Expect it to challenge your growth, requiring your
advancement and maturity. We get His wisdom in order to
use it, not so we can forget and have to ask for the same
things all over again.

Jesus alluded to our need to apply wisdom and grow in
the Parable of the Talents.

> *"Again, it will be like a man going on a
> journey, who called his servants and entrusted
> his wealth to them. To one he gave five bags of
> gold, to another two bags, and to another one
> bag, **each according to his ability....**"*

*Matthew 25:14, 15 NIV (Author's emphasis)*

The servants all received an amount based on what the
master believed they could handle. The wiser of the servants
applied what they knew to what they were given and
doubled up while the servant, later called wicked, passively
sat still and fear gripped him. The master did not provide a
step-by-step guide for the wicked servant, so he did nothing
and received his just reward.

Even when we are hearing clearly from the Holy Spirit,
we will still have matters to consider, circumstances to
unravel and hard work to do as we sort through options. We
will need to seek the advice of others and weigh it out with
what we know and what has been revealed. This is not
punishment. It's part of the reward and responsibility of
greater trust in the kingdom.

# WHEN THINGS SEEM QUIET, TAKE THE NEXT STEP

Part of the maturing process requires us to experience the times of change and growth. We get comfortable in a place where guidance is easier to hear or apply, and then we are beckoned to another place. In the transition God may seem silent.

In my experience, and from the accounts of many who have walked this road much longer, **times of quiet are usually times for our obedient action.** There are steps in front of us we know we need to take, but maybe we're waiting for more clarity or direction before proceeding.

When our next step is revealed it's important for us to take it. God knows us better than we do and will not show us more than we need for that moment. In my own life there are many times I may not have taken the first step had I known what the second step was going to be ahead of time.

It's likely Abraham would not have followed God into unknown lands if he knew his son would be asked of him. Moses might have flatly refused to lead the Exodus if God had shown him all he would have to endure. I am confident Gideon would have stayed hidden in the winepress if the Lord had shared His battle plan of 300 guys with clay pots. Our Father's wisdom exceeds ours and we must obey what is clearly revealed even if it isn't as much as we would like to see.

Peter's deliverance from prison in Acts 12 gives us great insight to God's timing and revelation. I'm sure Peter had prayed and asked for his chains to be taken off many times as he sat awaiting certain execution; however, it was not until the angel showed up and said, "Get up!" that the chains fell off (12:7).

The sequence that follows feels familiar to me for some reason. I can only imagine myself in that circumstance and how funny my questions might have been. "Awesome! Thanks for getting those chains off... now how am I gonna get out? There are guards all along the way and what about that gate? It's huge!"

If my patterns in the past are any indication, I would have wanted to know how to accomplish each step before taking the first one. Praise God I've been delivered from that! (For the most part...)

Maybe Peter still had a little of that in him too, because he was only given one step at a time. As he obeyed, the next step was revealed. It was as if the angel was getting a five-year old ready for school.

"Get up!" Peter gets up. "Put on your clothes and sandals." Peter does. "Wrap your cloak around you and follow me." Away they go (12:8, 9). Then watch what happened!

They walked past one guard and another. Then they reached the iron gate only to see it swing open on its own (12:10). Could God have dealt with the guards and opened the gate before He even woke Peter up? Yes, but in His wisdom, nothing happened until Peter faced them. Each next step and provision was revealed as the previous steps were taken.

True to form, and like so many of us, Peter didn't realize he had been guided and delivered by the Lord until it was over! (12:11)

I've prayed for countless doors to be opened in my life and none of them have ever opened until I reached them. Sometimes, too, I reached them and they still didn't open.

# THE CORRIDOR

Facing an unopened door is an interesting place to be. "Did I miss what You said God? Is there something else I'm supposed to do?" This is always a place of growth.

For me, that growth has usually come in terms of increased patience and trust. When I have confidence He has led me, I can trust Him to open the right doors at the right time. My personality has usually been very aggressive, though, and closed doors have represented something to be kicked down. Each time I've forced my way into or through a place where God has encouraged patience I have reaped heartache.

Just as with Peter, our responsibility is to trust and follow, knowing God takes care of the doors. **When we reach a closed door, it's okay to jiggle the handle or knock, but not to bust it down.** If it doesn't open look around and see if there's another door open nearby. If there isn't, maybe God is making something wonderful available to you while you wait in the corridor.

It's not always easy to wait and trust, but pleasing God has never been promoted as easy. Faith is an adventure and much harder work than most people throughout history have been willing to engage. **If it were not adventurous, we wouldn't need His guidance. But it is. And He gives it freely.**

# CHAPTER 13

# Packing for the Journey

★ ★ ★ ★ ★

The childhood memories that mean the most to me as a man are hunting or fishing expeditions with my dad. Whether floating and camping on the Gasconade River or disappearing into the woods to squirrel hunt all morning, I never really thought about having what I needed.

We might load up the canoe for a three-day float, in the age before cell phones, and I always trusted that we had everything we needed or it would be provided as we went. It was my Dad's job to get us packed and to know how to navigate to our destination.

When I began to load up with friends for my own floating adventures, I realized how much I took for granted. First I had to learn my way around — which river access to use and where it was — which landmarks gave me information about position and distance to my destination. There was much more to it than just climbing into the canoe and grabbing my fishing pole.

Once the navigation became easier to handle, I learned how to pack. I learned what were essentials for short trips and how the list expanded for longer voyages. I had to make sure I knew what was needed to make everything more enjoyable and to protect against unforeseen problems.

**I learned that progressing from just *being along for the journey* to *being responsible for the journey* was part of being a man.** If I wanted the adventure and the joy the journey provided, I had to know how to make it happen. I believe that's the message God has blessed me to share with you.

The progression from boyhood to authentic manhood is the most important transformation you'll ever make in Christ. There are full-grown, mature males in our world who have still not progressed out of boyhood. There are also many boys who are striving and succeeding in taking on the things of manhood. The transition is not automatic and must be approached as a matter of choice.

I used to think when my dad deemed me old enough to go on my own, I was ready. What I learned is that "ready" requires work and choice. We are saved by grace before we are ready to walk as mature Christians. Our daily choice to engage the elements of our *Manhood GPS* is what makes us ready and helps us mature.

With our GPS functioning as God designed, we tune our adventurous spirits to His infinite guidance. No more fear of being lost! We can pursue Him with all we are and know He is faithful to guide us as we journey together.

# THE OTHER HALF OF A GREAT ADVENTURE

Similar to our journeys in the natural, knowing where we are going in life is not the entire package. My ability to navigate down the river might be spot on, but the journey will be much harder and less enjoyable, if I don't pack correctly.

Our adventure through life requires us to bring a few things along. When I think of preparing for a trip I usually think of someone like Lewis and Clark, loading up before heading west. The provisions needed for an adventure so massive were huge. Fortunately for them, they were backed by the U.S. Government, which had a keen interest in their success. Nothing was spared to ensure they had what they needed.

As you set out on your journey, I want you to remember your starting point: In Christ, seated in heavenly places, at the right hand of the Father. You are in the seat of authority in the throne room of Heaven. Nothing you need will be withheld from you! God has a keen interest in your success and wants you to have everything.

In contrast to taking a natural trip, however, packing for the journey with God requires that you pack light. He brings what is needed when you need it. Packing light is our act of faith, believing He will provide. The things we take with us from the start and keep for the entire time are so useful and powerful they don't require much space.

# BELIEF

In the realm of faith, it might seem obvious to have belief as part of the packing list, but I am not referring to our belief in Jesus. This belief is in ourselves and what we can do with all the help Jesus promised us.

Jesus told His disciples belief in Him would produce some amazing things in their lives and by extension in our lives. *"Whoever believes in me will do the works I have been doing, and they will do even greater things than these"* (John 14:12 NIV). Greater than Jesus! That's so hard to grasp.

I've met few people who live as if they believe they can do greater works than Jesus. Any time we set out to do great things for God, the darkness comes against us and we begin to doubt. These are the essential times for having and knowing how to use faith.

A life in the kingdom requires us continually to go farther than we have before and to get out of our comfort zones regularly. I don't personally have anything against comfort zones. A comfort zone represents the things I've experienced and mastered. Anything I do within my comfort zone is a matter of knowledge and does not require belief. I know I can do it.

But to move outside of my comfort zone requires a different attitude and approach. I'm reminded of the scene in **The Lord of The Rings** when Sam and Frodo are leaving the Shire for their adventure. At one point, in the middle of field, Sam stops and says, "If I take one more step I will be the furthest away from home I've ever been." He was about to leave his comfort zone.

That place beyond the edge of your comfort zone requires belief. Yes, it might be similar to the places you have been before, but it is new. The farther you go, the more different and difficult it may become. Each step into new territory requires you to believe you can do it.

When you reach the place where your next step will take you farther than you've ever gone before, **believe**. Believe in the promises of Jesus. Believe the Holy Spirit is with you to guide you. Believe God will never call you on a journey for which He has not already equipped you.

You don't have to believe you can reach the mountaintop while standing at the bottom. Simply focus on the belief it requires to take the next step. Think of belief as your heavenly flashlight. The whole world around you can seem dark and scary, until you shine your light where you need to go. Wherever the light is, darkness cannot stay. When belief fills your heart and mind, fear has no place to stand.

# GRATITUDE

I'll never forget my first solo camping trip as a kid. The main reason being that I almost set out with no food. I've taken trips since then where I intentionally left without food for the purpose of having to provide for myself, but on my first trip it was not that way.

Proudly going through my packing list and checking things off, my friend asked me, "So how are you carrying your food? I don't see a cooler or anything."

Adventures of any sort are demanding and going without nourishment is unwise. We think it foolish to do so in the natural, but everyday, men are starving spiritually because they've forgotten a primary form of nourishment in the kingdom. Gratitude.

> *Give thanks to the Lord, for he is good; his love endures forever.*
>
> *1 Chronicles 16:34 NIV*

The theme of thanksgiving appears frequently throughout the Bible. It's how we're to enter His presence and give Him praise. Our society in general is very ungrateful and we fall too easily into their pattern. A feeling of entitlement isn't just a poor attitude among our youngest generation, *it's a deception.*

Adam and Eve were deceived with entitlement and lost touch with gratitude when satan got them to doubt God and to believe they could be their own source. Our spirits are nourished, and remembering God's goodness and being grateful for it enhance our warfare.

Many men I've spoken with through the years have a hard time finding gratitude. We've been indoctrinated as a gender to never be satisfied with what we have and to always strive for more. This fosters a false belief that somehow showing gratitude means we're not trying to improve, so we starve ourselves from appreciating what God is doing in our lives.

What many do not comprehend is how little gratitude it takes to provide all the nourishment we'll ever need. If all you can manage at the beginning of your journey is a little thanksgiving, even if it's forced, that's enough because of an exponential property within gratitude.

The instant we show gratitude it expands. You may only have a few crumbs, which wouldn't keep you going, but as soon as you allow them to enter your spirit, your capacity for gratitude grows. The more grateful you are, the more grateful you can become.

Don't make the mistake of thinking your gratitude will show up when big things happen. The dad who can't appreciate playing catch with his kids in the backyard will not suddenly find gratitude at Disney World. Thankfulness begins in the small things and the big things follow.

# FORGIVENESS

If gratitude is the nourishment that keeps us going, forgiveness is how we remove obstacles. Sin, guilt and resentment are the biggest roadblocks we face, and forgiveness is the only solution. Maybe you can get around them for a little while, but they never go away through avoidance.

God created, and Jesus fulfilled, the entire concept of forgiveness just for us. Not only so we could come into right relationship with Him, but also so we could be in right relationship with each other... and ourselves.

One thing that keeps us from packing forgiveness for the journey is a misunderstanding of what it is. The forgiveness we receive from God doesn't say the wrong things we've done are acceptable. God doesn't expect us to forgive each other by saying the wrong that was done to us was right. **Forgiveness will not change what is done; it will change how we respond.**

When we forgive, we lay down our right to see someone punished for what they've done. Forgetting an offense is tricky business for us, but deciding to drop our prosecution of the offense is more tangible.

I've found that most of us can forgive others much easier than we can forgive ourselves. More men are blocked in their spiritual journeys by guilt and regret than anything else. When you find yourself in this position, ask yourself a couple of questions.

- Was Jesus punished enough for my sin?

- If the God of the universe forgives me, who am I to withhold forgiveness from myself?

Holding on to guilt, resentment or bitterness is like carrying around a pack full of boulders. When forgiveness is available in ready amounts, we can move more freely and shake off weariness.

# ACTION

*In their hearts humans plan their course, but the Lord establishes their steps.*

*Proverbs 16:9 NIV*

Please note what this verse **doesn't** say: God takes them for us. **Part of the challenge facing modern Christianity is not a lack of knowledge, but a lack of action.**

For the sake of political correctness and popularity, most churchgoers watch passively while sin and perversion wash over our world. As men of God we must have a bias for action in moving the kingdom forward. Show your faith by your deeds (James 2:18).

By spending more personal time with the Lord, you'll begin to know how to act more in line with His will. That confidence will cause you to recognize opportunities for service and seize them. This is when we become the hands and feet of Jesus. This is the kingdom in action.

We have His eternal, infinite guidance and all of the resources we will ever need at our disposal. It's time to go!

Just one more briefing at the trailhead and our journey begins....

# CHAPTER 14

# The Send Off

★ ★ ★ ★ ★

Men were created for adventure. Part of God's first instruction to mankind was to *"fill the earth and subdue it"* (Genesis 1:28). Putting our feet in new places is in our DNA. Because the fall of man separated us from God, our adventurous spirits still call us out, but our natural sense of direction got us lost. But through the blood of Jesus and our confession of His lordship in our lives, we're reconciled to God and have access to His guidance.

By searching the Bible as we would a map, we gain more revelation of the nature and characteristics of **God**. When we spend time in **His presence**, our hearts are turned fully toward Him and our desires and destinations align with His will. And by receiving the **Holy Spirit,** we connect with the thoughts of God and are guided through spiritual growth and life decisions.

Take note of those primary components.

God

His Presence

The Holy Spirit

**God — Presence — Spirit. *GPS!***

How awesome is God to make something so far beyond us, so simple to comprehend and so easy to remember?

As we wrap up the preparation phase of our journey, it's important to give praise and honor to God for what He has given. The GPS of our natural world is incredible in many ways, but the GPS our Father has given is so much more. It's able to guide us through anything life may bring, while calling forward the authentic manhood He placed in us.

And that's the importance and purpose of the *Manhood GPS*. It will guide us into the fullness of manhood, which is the fullness of Christ. The Father wants His Son manifested on Earth through us! ***I hope that doesn't sound easy, because it's not.*** And I don't believe it's supposed to be. That's a misconception among some believers that has even gained popularity with cynics.

A life lived for God and in His service will not be easy. If all things were easy for believers, we wouldn't need divine guidance! By visiting our key scriptures one more time, our final thoughts on the *Manhood GPS* concept come full circle.

> *I have not stopped giving thanks for you, remembering you in my prayers. I keep asking that the God of our Lord Jesus Christ, the glorious Father, may give you the Spirit of wisdom and revelation, so that you may know him better. I pray that the eyes of your heart may be enlightened in order that **you may know the hope to which he has called you, the riches of his glorious inheritance in his holy people, and his incomparably great power for us who believe....***
>
> *Ephesians 1:16-19 NIV (Author's emphasis)*

*For this reason, since the day we heard about you, we have not stopped praying for you. We continually ask God to fill you with the knowledge of his will through all the wisdom and understanding that the Spirit gives, so that you may live a life worthy of the Lord and please him in every way: bearing fruit in every good work, growing in the knowledge of God, **being strengthened with all power according to his glorious might so that you may have great endurance and patience.***

*Colossians 1:9-11 NIV (Author's emphasis)*

Look at the end result of all the things we've discussed. We're given this GPS so we can **know hope, be reminded of our inheritance** and **lean on His incomparably great power.** Colossians is more to the point by revealing the purpose is **to strengthen us in God's glorious might** so **we can have endurance and patience**.

Endurance and patience aren't needed for a life of ease, but for a life of challenge and adventure! We live in a world bent on suppressing and eliminating authentic manhood; yet we're called to love that world as authentic, Christ-like men.

Our *Manhood GPS* is designed to give us guidance, endurance and patience. A life dedicated to God will often attract more trouble because it stands directly opposed to the enemy. Jesus said, *"In this world you will have trouble. But take heart! I have overcome the world"* (John 16:33 NIV).

Take heart. Have endurance. Be patient.

James gives us the full purpose of the trouble Jesus referred to and what our attitude should be toward it.

*Consider it pure joy, my brothers and sisters, whenever you face trials of many kinds, because you know that the testing of your faith produces perseverance. Let perseverance finish its work so that you may be mature and complete, not lacking anything.*

*James 1:2-4 NIV*

Why does a life lived for God attract trouble? Why do we have to face trials? Because God's wisdom will often allow things He could prevent, so we can receive something we need. He invites us to rejoice when the world comes against us, because Jesus has overcome the world and we are joined with Him. **Every time we face trouble with faith in God's sovereignty and love, we are going to receive something glorious. We will become more like Jesus.**

Your *Manhood GPS* will guide you on the best path — not necessarily the easiest. It will guide and protect you through the trials along the way. With your face set toward Heaven and heart turned toward God, no matter what the world brings, your trajectory is always up. Ultimately, your path leads to the throne of Christ where you will hear, "Well done good and faithful servant!"

So fire up your *Manhood GPS* and set out into the world — reflecting Christ in your day-to-day — bringing the Light of the World to the dark and mundane of earthly existence — drawing others to their own journey as you become a successful adventurer in the kingdom of God.

**Hopefully our paths will cross along the way.**

# About the Author

## PJ McCLURE

PJ McClure is a rising voice in the movement to resurrect authentic manhood. As a mentor to young and older men alike, PJ communicates kingdom principles through writing and speaking to businesses, churches and schools.

He is a servant of Jesus, husband, father, pastor and endorsed communicator for *FivestarMan*.

# Contact Information

For more resources or to schedule PJ McClure for
your church, business, conference or a personal consultation

## PLEASE CONTACT:

**PJ McClure**
The Mindset Maven, LLC
4248 Hwy 83
Bolivar, MO 65613
*PJMcClure.com*

## FLIP THE S.W.I.T.C.H.

One of the world's most used, yet least explained buzzwords is *Mindset*.
Everyone wants the right mindset, but no one has ever laid out exactly
how to get it. Until now...

After fourteen years of studying the most successful people throughout
history, thousands of interviews and ground-breaking revelation from the
Holy Spirit, PJ McClure demystifies *mindset* with his book, **Flip The
S.W.I.T.C.H.: *How To Turn On And Turn Up Your Mindset.***

An Amazon bestseller, sold in more than twenty countries, **Flip The
S.W.I.T.C.H.** could be the key to your breakthrough!

Order **Flip The S.W.I.T.C.H.** today in print or audio at *PJMcClure.com*.

www.ingramcontent.com/pod-product-compliance
Lightning Source LLC
Chambersburg PA
CBHW071952100426
42736CB00043B/3018